# Anxiety and Depression

## A NATURAL APPROACH

# Anxiety and Depression

## A NATURAL APPROACH

Shirley Trickett

Ulysses Press  Berkeley, CA

2001

Copyright © 1997, 2001 Shirley Trickett. All rights reserved under International and Pan-American Copyright Conventions, including the right to reproduce this book or portions thereof in any form whatsoever, except for use by a reviewer in connection with a review.

Published by: Ulysses Press
P.O. Box 3440
Berkeley, CA 94703
www.ulyssespress.com

Library of Congress Catalog Card Number: 00-102270

ISBN: 1-56975-226-5

First published as *Coping With Anxiety and Depression* by Sheldon Press

Printed in Canada by Transcontinental Printing

10 9 8 7 6 5 4

Update Author: Joanna Pearlman
Editor: Mark Woodworth
Cover Design: Sarah Levin, Leslie Henriques
Cover Illustration: "Seated Woman" by Diana Ong/SuperStock
Editorial and production staff: Lily Chou, Lindsay Mugglestone,
    Steven Zah Schwartz, Marin Van Young
Indexer: Sayre Van Young

Distributed in the United States by Publishers Group West
and in Canada by Raincoast Books

This book has been written and published strictly for informational purposes, and in no way should it be used as a substitute for consultation with your medical doctor or health care professional. All facts in this book came from medical files, clinical journals, scientific publications, personal interviews, published trade books, self-published materials by experts, magazine articles, and the personal-practice experiences of the authorities quoted or sources cited. You should not consider educational material herein to be the practice of medicine or to replace consultation with a physician or other medical practitioner. The author and publisher are providing you with information in this work so that you can have the knowledge and can choose, at your own risk, to act on that knowledge. The author and publisher also urge all readers to be aware of their health status and to consult health professionals before beginning any health program, including changes in exercise or dietary habits. **Be sure to tell your doctor and pharmacist about *all* medications you take, both prescription drugs and over-the-counter products such as vitamins and supplements. Some herbs (even some teas) and supplements may interact with prescribed medications.**

All names and identifying characteristics of real persons have been changed in the text to protect their confidentiality.

*For my children, Helen, David, and Sarah,*
*who love me in spite of being on the receiving end*
*of all my inexperience.*

# Contents

# *Foreword*

When I first met Shirley Trickett I was at medical school, learning that tranquilizers were an effective, safe, and nonaddictive treatment for anxiety. Of course, like any good medical student, I believed it. When Shirley told me that she thought that these drugs were addictive, I was naturally rather skeptical and said, politely, that the medical world might listen when she had hard evidence to prove her case. Far from being discouraged by the indifference of the medical profession, not to mention overly opinionated medical students, she set about gathering that evidence, while at the same time getting on with the job of helping people to deal with their problems in ways other than taking drugs. She has been instrumental in a campaign that has alerted doctors to the dangers of tranquilizers and, in the process, she has acquired an expertise in the management of anxiety problems that is second to none.

Some years have passed since Shirley first bent my ear about tranquilizers, and a new generation of medical students is learning that tranquilizers are dangerous, addictive, and ineffective in the treatment of anxiety. Her opinions, once medical heresy, have become medical fact. Her first book, *Coming Off Tranquillizers and Sleeping Pills* (published by Ulysses Press under the title *Free Yourself from Tranquilizers and Sleeping Pills*), has become essential reading not just for those trying to find a new life without drugs like Ativan and Valium, but also for doctors like myself, who have to deal with such problems in the course of their work. I regularly recommend Shirley's first book to my patients when they ask about tranquilizer addiction, and their reaction is usually: "This is amazing, Doctor; I could have written it myself. It's exactly how I feel."

Now that tranquilizers have fallen from favor and the medical profession is trying to undo the damage of more than 20 years mistakenly prescribing them, we have found ourselves with little alternative treatment to offer patients suffering from anxiety or "milder" forms of depression. Fortunately, while we had been seeking chemical answers to emotional problems and encouraging patients to believe these were possible, people like Shirley had been looking for other ways of dealing with anxiety and depression. This hard-earned knowledge is now finding its way into psychiatric practice with good effect. More importantly, we are now seeing a climate emerging in which people are showing a greater interest in their psychological welfare and a greater willingness to seek the solution to their problems on their own or in self-help groups.

This book, written with the clarity and insight that made *Coming Off Tranquillizers and Sleeping Pills* such a great success, tackles the problems of anxiety and depression with a compassion that springs from first-hand experience and an expertise that has come from a receptiveness to new ideas that my own profession would do well to learn from. I am sure that *Anxiety and Depression: A Natural Approach* will take its place alongside *Coming Off Tranquillizers* in offering hope to those who suffer from the misery of these conditions and at the same time providing excellent practical guidance to health care professionals working in this field.

Dr. J. W. McDonald
Registrar in Psychiatry, Rainhill Hospital
Prescott, Merseyside, U.K.

## *Caution*

This book is not a substitute for professional help. Before using self-help methods, you are advised to take your health problems to your physician.

The author and publisher welcome your comments and suggestions for future editions. We would also appreciate hearing how this book has helped you. Please write us at Ulysses Press, P.O. Box 3440, Berkeley, CA 94703. You may also send e-mail to readermail@ulysses press.com.

# PART ONE
## Understanding Anxiety
## and Depression

# CHAPTER ONE

# Anxiety, Depression, and the Whole Person

Since the publication of *Coming Off Tranquillizers and Sleeping Pills* (published as *Free Yourself from Tranquilizers and Sleeping Pills* in the United States), I have had many requests to write more about anxiety and depression. Throughout the United States, most state or local health departments provide treatment for people suffering from severe psychiatric disorders, but do very little for what is considered to be less severe nervous illness: mild to moderate states of anxiety and depression. This may be the way these conditions are described, though there is rarely anything mild or moderate about the degree of misery involved. The symptoms are often severe, protracted, and very frightening. I hope that what follows in this book will help and encourage those who feel defeated and degraded by nervous troubles.

The conventional approach to the nervously ill so often fails because only part of the person is looked at. Unless body, mind, and spirit are all nurtured, full recovery cannot take place. Homing in on just one problem is like painting the same section of the Golden Gate Bridge over and over again. No matter how much the paint gleams in the treated part, it will not stop rust developing elsewhere, making the whole structure unstable.

As medicine gets more and more specialized, it seems to retreat from the all-around common-sense approach of the old days. We are losing something very valuable here. Each professional "hat" is firmly tied on, sometimes with a brim so low it partly obscures vision, and the therapist does not see anything outside his or her discipline. Take Mary, for example. She is seeing her psychiatrist regularly; she finds him helpful, but would make much better progress if only he would open his eyes and see her physical needs too. Her mouth is always covered in herpes (cold sores) and she is painfully thin. Her psychiatrist is so bound up in her neurosis that he does not see the rest. This happens in all areas of medicine. When the nurse from the home health care service visits John, for example, she is so busy dressing his leg and filling him full of antibiotics, she does not see how much he is grieving for his wife. Or, the overworked counselor at the community health center who sees Robert but doesn't have time to explore whether his needs are really being met; his death phobia will not respond to tranquilizers, and instead he needs to be given a loving dose of hope and to be taught how much he is damaging his nerves by his hectic daily routine. The clinic, while it readily prescribes pills, might have to follow strict treatment guidelines and forbid its staff to give this kind of personalized care.

This book is for the nervous person as a whole: aching body, confused mind, and wearied spirit. Its goal is to explain in a simple way some of the causes of anxiety and depression and, by discussing the symptoms, help you to identify whether it is anxiety or depression, or a mixture of the two, that is making you feel so ill.

It also stresses the importance of learning how to love and accept yourself just as you are and realize there is no shame or blame attached to being nervously ill—it can happen to anyone. The nervous system is not separate—somewhere outside of you; rather, it's right in there with the bones, muscles, skin, and other parts of your body. If your body or mind has more stress than it can take, then it hurts your nerves. It's as simple as that.

Part One deals with understanding the causes and problems in anxiety and depression, and discusses their treatments, both medicinal and nonmedicinal. Part Two, the self-help section, shows how you can work with your body instead of pushing against it. Learning to think positively, practicing relaxation and controlled breathing techniques, and improving your eating habits are some of the ways you can help yourself. Self-help therapy can also work very well with professional medical or psychological help. They do not exclude each other. Many doctors and therapists nowadays encourage people to seek information and be more responsible about themselves.

Although there are many words used for nervous illness—affective disorder, anxiety, depression, mood disorder, neurosis, nervous breakdown, and so on—they all refer to the same thing: tired nerves. And tired nerves can recover, *if* they are given the chance.

No matter how long you have been nervously ill, you *can* recover and find peace and joy in life. Be prepared to accept that it will take time, and that there will be ups and downs—nature does not heal in a straight line.

While the symptoms on the following pages may be only too familiar and seem unimportant, all persistent symptoms must be investigated. Consult your doctor if you have not already done so. If you are told "It's only your nerves," then self-help could change your life.

# CHAPTER TWO

# What Is Anxiety?
# What Is Depression?

## What Is Total Health?

True health is not just absence of symptoms. It is characterized by feeling physically well, being self-reliant, having the ability to adjust to change, and demonstrating a sense of responsibility for oneself. This entails developing insight into one's own feelings and actions, and also cultivating a degree of self-worth that can stand on its own without the good opinion of others.

## What Is Nervous Illness?

The most common symptoms of nervous illness are anxiety and depression, conditions that can occur alone or together. The feelings they produce range from mild tension or being "down" or "blue," to symptoms so disabling that a normal life is not possible.

## What Is Anxiety?

The word anxiety comes from a Latin word meaning "worried about the unknown," and is also related to a Greek word meaning "compress or strangle." Are you being strangled by anxiety? Anxiety is a reaction to living in the world. It is as much part of our world as eating. It has been here since we humans began to walk upright. It is normal. How can we escape it, since it starts with the trauma of birth?

## Let Us Daydream

If it were possible to be conceived with love, in a clean trouble-free environment, and to spend our days in utero happily splashing around inside a serene, well-nourished mother, this would be a good start for a trouble-free journey. If it were also possible to slide painlessly through the birth canal to arrive in a gentle world, free from harsh lights and noises that assault our senses; and if we were received into warm water by our parents, and not upended by the buttock-slapping hands (the first injustice!) of masked strangers, this would be another step in the right direction.

And if we held a guarantee from God or our own personal divine force, saying, "You will be loved with a love that sets you free; you will be disciplined with gentleness; and, after long years of happiness and fulfillment, you will leave this life as painlessly as you entered it," then anxiety would not be normal.

You can see it is impossible not to have some degree of anxiety. The aim is not to fight fear continually, but rather to live happily alongside it by learning how to reduce it to manageable proportions. If you are ashamed of being anxious, then you are ashamed of being a human being and having a body. We experience the world through our bodies.

## Is Anxiety Necessary?

When we are afraid, chemical changes in our bodies take place that increase the energy levels and enable us to respond to the danger or threat, and take quick action—either by defending ourselves (for example, fighting off an attempted attacker) or by escaping the danger (such as running away from a charging bull). The "fight or flight" response to real danger has helped humans survive from the very beginning. The trouble starts if we cannot switch off this extra energy when it is not needed; the body fails to adjust and we become "wound up." This useless state is rather like leaving the car engine running for 24 hours when you only need it running for two short journeys daily. In the same way as the gas is wasted and the tank runs down to empty, our energy is wasted, our nervous system is depleted, and we eventually become ill.

## What Is Depression?

Depression is an illness of the feelings. It ranges from an overreaction to normal sadness, to gray nothingness where you are still just able to function, to utter despair, hopelessness, and prostration. In severe depression even the bodily functions are affected.

## Is Depression Necessary?

In anxiety, the activity of both body and mind is speeded up. In depression, they are both slowed down. Depression often follows anxiety —it forces us to rest; this could be its function. Although this slowing down can be useful, if it goes on too long you need to do something about it.

It will be easier to understand how we become anxious and depressed if you first learn how the nervous system works. This we deal with in the next chapter.

# CHAPTER THREE

# Understanding the Nervous System

The nervous system is the network of communication between various parts of the body, a little like a telephone exchange with the brain as the central switchboard, the spine as the main cable, and the nerves as the telephone lines that carry messages. It is divided into two systems: the central system and the autonomic system.

## The Central Nervous System

This controls voluntary movement and is responsible for all sensations in muscles, bones, and joints. It is under the control of the will—you want to pick up a pen, so you reach out your hand and do so. The central nervous system works well unless it is neurologically impaired or, in times of terror, paralyzed with fear.

## The Autonomic Nervous System

This system controls all involuntary muscles—internal organs, blood vessels, and so on. The autonomic nervous system is under the control of the emotions; for example, anger will cause your blood pressure to rise, while fear will make the stomach churn. It has two parts: the sympathetic system, which has a stimulating effect, and the parasympathetic system, which has a calming effect.

When your parasympathetic nervous system does not work properly, you become overanxious.

Think of the sympathetic nervous system as a race-car driver in a red Ferrari speeding down the track at 175 miles per hour. By contrast, think of the parasympathetic nervous system as someone puttering slowly down the road in an old blue Volkswagen. All the internal organs are governed by the sympathetic nervous system and have two sets of nerves, one stimulating, the other quieting.

## The Sympathetic Nervous System—Go, Go, Go!

Imagine a firefighter going to knock down a fire. His nervous system is "sympathetic" to his emotions and prepares his body to fight for survival. It does this in response to his tightening his muscles and (unconsciously) squeezing his glands and, rather like squeezing oranges, it produces "juice," a chemical called adrenaline. As a result, his blood pressure rises, his heart rate speeds up, his breathing becomes rapid (he needs more oxygen because he is rushing around), and he sweats to cool himself. To help him even more, his blood is diverted from his abdomen to his legs so that he can run faster. (This is the reason for that sinking feeling in the stomach when we are afraid.) With a reduced blood supply to his digestive organs, he does not think of food, or of the need to go to the bathroom. So when his sympathetic nervous system is in action, his adrenaline/anxiety levels are high.

Do you see that his body is behaving very much like that of an overanxious person, with rapid breathing and pulse, sweating, churning emotions, and so forth? The difference is that he is using his anxiety productively, and in fact there is something for him to worry about. If he had been very fearful, and if he had not used the extra adrenaline, he could have become so tense that he vomited and emptied the contents of his bowel and bladder (inelegantly but accurately called "scared shitless"). This may be a primitive mechanism for making the body lighter to enable it to run faster.

How does the firefighter get back to normal adrenaline levels? When the fire is out and the danger is over, the firefighter sits in the hook-and-ladder truck on the way back to the station, and as he relaxes his tight muscles, different chemicals are released to give the opposite effect to adrenaline. This is the parasympathetic system working efficiently: his blood pressure drops, his heart rate and breathing slow down, he stops sweating, the blood comes back into his abdomen from his arms and legs. He realizes he is hungry, and starts thinking about food. He is also conscious that he needs to go to the bathroom. He feels relaxed, his muscles are comfortable. So his adrenaline/anxiety levels are low.

It is easy to see from this why the nerves get exhausted. Repeated stresses, conscious and unconscious (even small stresses), keep us in a state of red alert all the time. It's like the firefighter rushing around with hoses and ladders long after the fire is out. He wants to slow down but he *can't*. His adrenaline (and therefore anxiety) levels are still too high.

Have you ever been so wound up that you continued working long after you needed to—even though you were exhausted? Chapter Four tells you how to slow down and get off the racetrack.

# How to Get Off the Racetrack

## Working with the Parasympathetic Nervous System

Since this slowing-down part of the nervous system responds to the emotions, it would seem sensible to say to yourself: "There is absolutely nothing to make me so fearful—calm down, stop sending out so much adrenaline, I don't need it!" Unfortunately, a brain flooded with adrenaline does not listen to reason, for instead it is obeying the chemical messengers that are telling it to speed up and stay on the racetrack. The best first-aid treatment is to use the body to calm down. You can eventually learn to use breathing and relaxation techniques, training your body to obey your commands anywhere you are. Self-talk is also very useful in the long term, but in a panic situation it is not very effective. You need to do mechanically what your parasympathetic system (the slow one) should be doing automatically. It is a bit like having to ask a friend to give your car a push-start when you find your battery's dead. Your relaxation response is not in good working order and needs to be retrained.

## Remember What Made the Firefighter Relax

If the muscles relax, then the chain reaction for the relaxation response is set in motion. You may not be able to do this at will, because you are so "uptight" (a perfect term for one whose nerves are drawn up tensely)—but by slowing down your breathing you can reduce the amount of oxygen getting to your brain, thereby getting off the racetrack and coaxing your parasympathetic system to take over. This is fully described in a later chapter.

## "I Can't Be Bothered with This—I Want an Instant Cure"

Some anxious people get irritated when it is suggested that they can train their bodies not to be on "red alert" all the time. They want an instant cure for the dreadful feelings of panic—a pill or an injection, a magic bullet. They often get annoyed when it is suggested that their bodies are responsible for the feelings. They prefer to think the "jitters" descend out of nowhere and have nothing to do with them at all.

The truth is that, yes, they have no *conscious* part in it, but they fail to realize that their symptoms are caused by their nervous system being weakened by repeated strain—not only from the present life stresses, but also from the stored pain in the *unconscious*. (When pain is mentioned in this book it will mean emotional pain: sadness, grief, anger, frustration, loneliness, and the like, unless physical pain is specifically mentioned.)

Happily, most people are eager to learn how to use their bodies in a way that will allow the nerves to heal. Confidence grows as they begin to see the results. Many say such things as: "My life is still full of problems, but I can feel my body reacting differently now."

## It's Worth the Effort

Are you willing to continue to be bullied by your unconscious into using tension as a response to stress—*or* are you eager to enroll in the "get along better with your nerves school" and do the boring work necessary to feel more in charge of your life?

The methods described in this book are safe, cheap (in fact, often free), and effective. They are also sometimes a chore to do, and time-consuming! Some people have said that it feels like self-absorption to be continually watching yourself. But the goal is really to use self-interest productively as a means to an end. After all, it is better to be absorbed in the cure than in the symptoms. Anxious or depressed people are the first to admit, anyway, that they are preoccupied with their symptoms all the time.

# CHAPTER FIVE

# Learn More About Your Nerves

People reading the following list of nervous symptoms often have several responses. The most common one is: "I was pleased to see all those things written down—I thought I was imagining them." Because people are often pessimistic when their nerves are in trouble, sometimes they lament: "Oh dear, I have so many of the symptoms on this list I must be having a breakdown." But if they could change it to: "I have quite a few of these symptoms, so it's time I took more care of myself," they would make a much speedier recovery. Worrying over the symptoms can perpetuate the illness.

## What Does It Feel Like to Be Overanxious?

Because the whole body is stimulated, everything is speeded up. This can result in: an increase in movement; thoughts being multiplied alarmingly; incessant and rapid speech; insomnia (difficulty sleeping); and also a speeding up of many of the functions of the body, such as heart rate, breathing, and the rate at which solid foods and liquids go through the digestive tract. Hence the need to go to the bathroom so often.

# What Are Nervous Symptoms?

- Feeling constantly exhausted
- No interest in life
- Panic attacks
- Irritability
- Lack of concentration
- Attention-seeking
- Hyperactivity
- Rapid speech
- Rushing thoughts
- Compulsive eating
- Paranoia (feeling persecuted)
- Irrational fears (phobias)
- Feelings of gloom and doom
- Suicidal feelings
- Restlessness
- Compulsive behavior
- Obsessional behavior
- Impotence, loss of interest in sex
- Tight chest or throat
- Swallowing problems
- Shaking
- Dizziness
- Diarrhea
- Gas
- Insomnia (sleep difficulty)
- Breathing difficulties
- Palpitations
- Excessive sweating
- Loss of appetite, weight loss
- Headaches
- Tinnitus (ringing in the ears)
- Aching all over

With all this to cope with, it is not surprising that the behavior of the person who has become overanxious changes. Relatives become very upset when the person they know as loving and easygoing becomes irritable, suspicious, and generally exhausting to be with. But it must be remembered that sufferers are not choosing this behavior and are often also bewildered and frightened by their angry and sometimes evil thoughts, as well as by the thoughtless actions they are inflicting on those they love.

In the rest of this chapter we explain some of the most distressing of these symptoms. Understanding what causes them is the first step in regaining control of your life.

## Feelings of Gloom and Doom

All the feelings caused by being overanxious are unpleasant, but the hardest to cope with are the wayward thoughts that become distorted and gloomy. For example, when you are well, if your husband is five minutes late home from work you would think he was held up in rush-hour traffic; when you are overanxious, you are convinced he is lying injured under a ten-ton truck. Health phobias are also very common. Every minor disorder is thought to be heart trouble or cancer. It can also turn an uneasy feeling into a full-blown panic attack. For example, normally when you are in a crowded place you might think: "I'll be glad to get out of here." When you are overanxious, you can become terror-stricken in the same situation and be convinced you are seriously ill: "I must get home, I am going to die/be sick/lose control." Panic attacks and how to cope with them are discussed below. (Also see *Panic Attacks: A Natural Approach*, by the author [Ulysses Press, 1999].)

## Suicidal Feelings

When anxiety levels are very high, it is common to have suicidal feelings. These feelings of hopelessness usually disappear as the anxiety levels come down, but it is essential to see your doctor if you are having this experience. **Suicide prevention hotlines are always there and ready to help.** Do not hesitate to contact them even if you know you would not act on the feelings. Many people say: "I had these awful suicidal feelings but I didn't feel I could call a hotline because I knew I wouldn't do anything. I feel so ashamed of these feelings; I have a lovely partner and family and can't see any reason for the way I feel." The telephone operator will give you the number if you can't concentrate enough to find it in the phone book.

## "It's My Agoraphobia—It's My Panic Attacks"

Sometimes people see suicidal feelings, panic attacks, or agoraphobia (fear of being out in public places, particularly alone) as an illness in itself. It often takes a lot to convince them that although it may be the worst effect they are experiencing, in fact it is only *part* of the story and will disappear as the anxiety levels come down. It is a little like seeing the cough in someone with bronchitis as the illness itself; the cough would not be there if the lungs were not congested. In the same way, the panic, agoraphobia, and other anxious feelings would not be there if the anxiety (adrenaline) levels were normal.

## Panic Attacks

Even reading about panic attacks makes some people feel nervous, so remember that you might be causing yours by simply going too long without food, or by breathing badly or inefficiently. More about these in Chapters Sixteen and Seventeen.

Panic attacks are characterized by sudden intense feelings of anxiety, often associated with feelings of impending death or disaster and fear of going mad. Unpleasant physical feelings are also present, including:

- Palpitations, pounding heartbeat
- Dizziness
- Nausea
- Shaking
- Choking sensations

- Feelings of unreality
- An urgent need to go to the bathroom
- Feeling "on pins and needles"
- Hot and cold flushes over the whole body

The attacks can last seconds or minutes or, more rarely, hours. In many ways, a panic attack is worse than being in a frightening situation; at least in the latter you know what the danger is, and when it is over you feel relief, and presumably know how to avoid getting into that situation again. In a panic attack, you are afraid of the feelings and even more afraid of the cause—because you don't know what it is. That is why most people think they are seriously ill or even that it is the end of the world. Fear of the fear takes over.

## Are Panic Attacks a Danger to Your Health?

Panic attacks are not a danger to your health, and once you recognize them for what they are—just a flood of adrenaline that makes you feel awful—they can be knocked down to size and conquered. How to cope with panic is described on page 107.

## When Do Panic Attacks Happen?

Here are three typical examples:

- I was sitting reading when I was gripped with the most awful feeling—a mixture of fear and sadness. I had never experienced anything like it before. The urge to move was overwhelming and I started to pace around the room. My wife tried to reassure me by saying it was only exhaustion. I felt quite irritated; such dreadful feelings could only be a stroke or heart attack. It completely obliterated my normal reactions; I could see I was alarming her but felt no concern. It passed after a few minutes, but the fear of its happening again lingered for several days. I felt better when my wife's friend gave me a clipping from a magazine. It said if you were run-down and missed meals you could have a panic attack, and it described exactly what I had felt. On the day it happened I had worked through lunch with only a cup of coffee and Ann was about to serve dinner when the feelings started.

• The first attack came when I was in the supermarket. I was reaching for an apple when the most awful feeling came over me; it was a mixture of a feeling of terrible loss and fear that something was going to happen. Everything seemed unreal. Fear of losing control overwhelmed me—I felt hot and sick and my legs were like jelly. I left the full shopping cart and rushed home. The feeling only lasted a few minutes. I felt like such a fool when I thought about the shopping. The next couple of days were a bit dreary and then I seemed fine. It happened again two weeks later in the library. Eventually I had to go to the doctor because I was afraid to go out alone. My husband had to drive me to work in our car (I usually take the subway), and I took a taxi home. I told my colleagues my "back" was troubling me.

• The doctor said my nerves were worn out and I needed to take two weeks' sick-leave. She knew me well enough to say I was not to use the time to landscape my garden or paint the house. I have had a very stressful life, but have always seen myself as having nerves of steel— I'm a "doer." I felt quite upset when I left the doctor's office with a note for my boss, a sheet on diet and nutrition (I had been doing a lot of "comfort" eating), and orders to rest and reorganize my life into a quieter routine. The doctor had scared me into following her instructions by saying that if I did not slow down I could have a nervous breakdown—*me!* I thought only thin, jittery people have breakdowns. I can see now there was part of me that was afraid to stop. Rushing around prevented me from looking at what was going on inside. There was also the fear that if I stopped, perhaps I wouldn't be able to get started again. It reminded me of when my son was young. We had walked the long way home. I asked him if he'd like to sit on the grass for a rest. His reply was, "No, Mommy. All the tiredness will come out and I won't be able to get up again."

## Can Panic Attacks Happen if You Are Not Nervously Exhausted?

The answer is "yes," but there will always be some underlying anxiety either from the past or present, as in the next example.

◆ My company, a local TV station, was sending me to Italy for three weeks to prepare a story. I felt delighted and made preparations for the trip. When I was in the travel agent's office, a few uneasy thoughts about the flight crept in. I wanted to talk to someone about it but felt like an idiot. When you are a professional broadcast anchorperson who frequently does stories about travel and the aerospace industry, it is quite hard to tell your friends you are anxious about flying.

I felt sure I would be all right when the time came, and so I pushed it to the back of my mind. Two weeks before the flight I woke up in the middle of the night in a terrible state. I was scared stiff, my heart was racing, and I felt confused. Convinced it was some terrible virus, I called the doctor for an emergency visit. When I arrived and talked for a few minutes, he was kind and said he could see I was distressed but after a few tests could find nothing physically wrong with me. He explained that I had experienced a panic attack, caused by the fear of the flight nagging away in my unconscious. He said he had a lot of patients who were panicky before trips. I was not convinced but took the two pills he offered me, one for each leg of the journey.

I had the same feeling but not as dramatically while I was in the check-in line at the airport, so he must have been right. I was glad to take one of his pills. The journey was fine; I did not need one on the return trip and I have not had a panic attack since. That was two years ago.

## Obsessions

What we call obsessions are persistent thoughts or images that the sufferer feels powerless to dismiss, even though he recognizes them as unpleasant, futile, or ridiculous.

Mild obsessions are common even in healthy people; a line of a song or part of an old conversation might go around and around in your head, or a silly idea like, "I'll fail my exam unless I wear green-and-yellow striped socks."

When these fixed ideas fill the mind and preoccupy the person so much that it disrupts his life, the condition is called obsessional neurosis, and professional help is needed. If the obsessions get to this stage, then it is usually an indication that the sufferer has been under a nervous strain for some time.

# Compulsions

When the anxiety caused by obsessive thoughts becomes severe, the sufferer changes his behavior in an attempt to cope. This is called compulsive behavior: actions, or avoidance of actions, that don't make sense either to the sufferer or to onlookers. The innocent childhood form of this could be such behaviors as avoiding stepping on lines in the pavement ("step on a crack, you'll break your mother's back!"), or tapping the forehead three times before entering the classroom. It's quite common for children to develop these little rituals—perhaps it's their way of feeling they have some magical control over a scary world.

## *Common Compulsive Acts*

These can include: continually checking—going back several times to make sure the stove has been turned off, or that the door has been locked. The person *knows* she has turned it off, but as soon as she moves away her anxiety rises again and she feels the need to check again. Sometimes a pattern develops and her anxiety will subside if she checks a specific number of times. Life can be exhausting and frustrating when you have to make seven trips from the front door to the kitchen before you can leave the house, or five trips from the gate to the front door to check that it has been locked.

Hand washing, cleaning of certain items, counting things, or continually tidying are other common rituals. As the anxiety levels come down, these distressing symptoms ease. Susan might say of her friend Penny, "She has an obsession about germs; she is always cleaning her house." Maybe Penny *does* spend a lot of time on what appears to be unnecessary housework, but if it is only part of a full life and she is happy and relaxed, then it is unlikely to be obsessive behavior. If, on the other hand, she thought about nothing *but* cleaning and germs and was unable to live a normal life, then this would be obsessional neurosis.

# Phobias

We have seen that anxiety is a mix of emotions we feel when threatened. A phobia is an intense fear of a situation or object that would not normally worry other people (except, of course, those who suffered from the same phobia).

It is possible to develop a phobia about any situation or object in life, animate or inanimate. Phobias about situations where there could possibly be some danger, such as thunderstorms, heights, snakes, or spiders are often easier to understand; but the more bizarre ones like fear of feathers, buttons, or walking past a hole in the road, are often observed with scorn—"Don't be stupid, how could anyone be so scared of buttons?"

It is important to realize that the terror experienced by the sufferer is the same whether his or her phobia concerns thunderstorms or encountering a woman in a green hat. Even the *thought* of the feared situation can cause a panic attack.

## *The Most Common Phobias*

*Situations*   Heights, enclosed spaces, the dark, being away from home

*Illness*   Cancer, heart trouble, losing a limb

*Animals*   Any animal, insect, or bird (even ones never likely to be encountered); even a picture or mental image may provoke terror

*Social*   Fear of meeting people either socially or in public, on buses, at a store, at the beauty shop, and so on

You might say we could all be afraid of some items in the above list. This is true, but it would not be a phobia unless our lives were completely disrupted by needing to avoid situations where the fear could be triggered—for example, being so afraid of dogs that you did not go out of the house at all, or not taking a job in a high-rise building because you were terrified to ride the elevator.

## Are You Ill if You Have a Phobia?

If your phobia were spiders and someone placed one on your arm, it would be a dreadful experience because of the chain reaction it would set up in your body—but this does not mean you are ill. You will learn later not only how to help your body after the event, but also how to prevent the phobia's being triggered by physical causes, such as hunger. Hypoglycemia is often mistaken for symptoms of phobia. To learn more about hypoglycemia, see Chapter Seventeen.

## Agoraphobia

Fear of leaving the safety of the home is probably the most common phobic problem. It can range from a mild fear of going out—into shops or traveling—to being completely housebound and severely anxious and depressed. Some people with agoraphobia seem to be especially sensitive to issues of separation and loss. Also, women are almost twice as likely to experience agoraphobia as are men. (Perhaps this can be attributed to society's greater acceptance—even encouragement—of avoidance coping strategies when used by women.)

## Treatment for Phobias

Phobias may persist for years, even decades, and were once thought to be very difficult to treat, even with medications. Tranquilizers, far from being a help, were found to be a source of phobic symptoms for many. But with the use of relaxation methods and breathing techniques, an increased awareness of the role diet plays in symptom management, and behavior modification (which may include progressive exposure treatment, also called *desensitization*), many people are being successfully treated.

Desensitization involves regular and progressive exposure to the feared situation. Exposure is done gradually as the sufferer faces his fear in stages. If the phobia were of cats, for instance, a person might first be shown pictures of cats, at the same time practicing relaxation and controlled breathing techniques. These skills could then be called on whenever he felt fear. He might next use visualization to imagine how he would feel being near a cat, and rehearse the encounter over and over in his mind. He may never learn to *like* cats, but he would progress (supported by his therapist) to being able to touch a cat without fear.

Some people do not need professional treatment to deal with their phobias. They may turn to self-help groups for support or to the encouragement of a family member or friend. To learn more about relaxation and breathing techniques, see Chapters Fifteen and Sixteen; Chapter Seventeen discusses dietary concerns.

## Hyperactivity

Hyperactivity is both a physical and a psychological problem. A common diagnosis in school-age American children, mostly boys, it is sometimes lumped with attention deficit disorder (ADD), and is known by the rather daunting term Attention Deficit Hyperactivity Disorder (ADHD). But hyperactivity is not limited to children. Adults can have it as well. When in this state, the person is so wound up with nervous energy that he is constantly on the move (hyperactive). The compulsion to move is overpowering. It can be productive when it is possible to harness it—working longer hours, for example—but it can also be aimless and associated with impulsive behavior and lack of concentration (attention deficit): "I can't settle; one minute I am in the garden planting bulbs, the next I am cleaning the oven, and then I am rushing around rearranging furniture. I never finish anything I start."

Hyperactivity is not only difficult to endure, it is also difficult to live with. Energy caused by severe tension bursts out all over and the sufferer cannot relax. Muscles ache and long for a rest, but the body will not allow it. Rapid thoughts and compulsive talking accompany hyperactivity.

Perhaps a visit to the doctor is in order to see if any physical problems —such as allergies—are causing the hyperactivity. Some hyperactive people find relief with prescribed medication. Meeting with a therapist is another possibility. Therapy may help a person reduce feelings of self-doubt and encourage productive and comfortable behavior. Beyond that, following the right diet, avoiding caffeine and sugary foods, exercising, and practicing relaxation and breathing techniques may aid in reducing excess energy.

## Lack of Concentration

Sometimes quite young people fear they are going senile because they cannot concentrate on reading, or even follow simple written instructions. They forget appointments and become very worried about losing their memory. It is often more likely that because they are so tense they have failed to take in the information, rather than that their memory has let them down. If you have difficulty concentrating, it may help to focus on one thing at a time and try to eliminate background noise (for instance, turn off the television if you're writing a letter). Also consider this a good time to take steps to simplify your life, especially your home environment. Reduce clutter as much as possible. Know that as the nerves recover, the concentration comes back. Meanwhile, why not write yourself a few reminders: "My concentration is poor because I am tense and don't sleep well—what am I going to do about it?" Or you might write this: "I think my hyperventilating is what's causing my lack of concentration."

## Insomnia

According to world-renowned sleep authority Dr. William Dement in his book *The Promise of Sleep* (see Further Reading and Reference on page 125), at least half of all humans acknowledge that they sometimes have trouble sleeping. Although you might find it comforting to know you are not the only one counting sheep at night, insomnia can be a particularly distressing symptom. When it occurs, there is no relief from the worries of the day, and you know you are going to feel tired and grumpy in the morning and have a hard time concentrating at work or school.

If it is a long-term problem, insomnia can cause depression. Some people find it difficult to go to sleep, while others wake up several times in the night or wake in the early hours of the morning. Disturbances include strange dreams, nightmares, panicky feelings, gas, or the need to pass urine frequently.

## What Causes Insomnia?

Many different factors may play a role in causing insomnia. The list is a long one, but causes of insomnia include worry, excitement, itching, pain, age, hormonal changes, diet, caffeine, alcohol, some medications, lack of exercise, not enough exposure to daylight, a poor sleep environment, and breathing or digestive problems. A healthy bowel seems to play a large part in getting a good night's sleep. Perhaps this is because the bacteria in the bowel produce chemicals that make us sleepy.

## Treatment for Insomnia

This is going to be a disappointing section for people expecting some simple solution to this problem. Regrettably, there isn't one. A disturbed night (unless it is for practical reasons like toothache or a crying baby) indicates that all is not well with your nerves, and until you look after them you will not get a good night's rest.

## Reset Your Internal Clock

Preparation for sleep starts when you get up in the morning. It is a great mistake to sleep late habitually in order to catch up on lost sleep. This disturbs the normal body rhythm; you miss the brightest time of the day and end up feeling jet lagged all the time. Even if you just slump at the kitchen table, do make the effort to get up, have breakfast, and keep to your routine. Try to get outside early and take a walk in the fresh air and sunlight. Limit caffeinated beverages to one or two cups in the morning, none after breakfast. The caffeine from one cup of coffee or tea can stay in your bloodstream for many hours before it is completely processed by enzymes in the liver. Some people find they are so sensitive to caffeine that they need to avoid it completely.

## Let Go of the Stresses of the Day

It is useless to rush about all day or even sit around the house in a tense state, and then expect your body to gear down half an hour before you want to go to sleep. So often the cry is, "I used to fall asleep the moment my head touched the pillow—what happened?"

Maybe your life is more hectic than it once was. To help calm yourself and prepare for sleep, turn off the television and computer at least an hour before bedtime. You may even want to try a "news fast"—as outlined by Dr. Andrew Weil in his book *Eight Weeks to Optimal Health* (see Further Reading and Reference on page 125). A news fast may not be easy. Some people are addicted to news programs and so-called "reality shows." Think about what this "mental junk food" adds to your life, aside from fulfilling a certain vicarious curiosity. You might use the time to write in a journal instead—this can be a good way to let go of the day's stresses.

## Create an Evening Ritual

The worst thing you can do is lie there worrying about not sleeping. Get up and move around. You could try some of the meditation exercises in Part Two, particularly slow breathing. Massaging the soles of the feet can be soothing. The heart rate can be slowed down by gentle pressure on the eyeballs. Also, you won't sleep if you are hungry. Have a snack and one of the nighttime herbal teas or some warm milk (excluding caffeine, of course). You may find it helpful to listen to relaxation tapes in bed; headphones cut out external noise and do not disturb your bed partner.

If you feel you are not making progress and want to break your present sleeping pattern, you could ask your doctor to prescribe a sleeping pill for two or three nights. If you'd rather not take sleeping pills, the following herbs or dietary modifications may be of help.

## Melatonin

Known as the "hormone of darkness," melatonin is a natural substance produced by the pineal gland in response to a decrease in the quantity of daylight entering through the eye. (Melatonin is what helps some animals hibernate through the long dark winter months.) The amount of melatonin in our bodies seems to vary over time. Children between the ages of one and three years old have the highest levels; the older we are, the less melatonin our bodies produce—which may be why insomnia increases as we age.

Melatonin does not *cause* you to sleep, but it does set the stage, informing your body that it is time to sleep. It has been shown to be a safe and effective way to reset the body's natural clock, and is especially useful to counter the effects of jet lag and shift work. Studies show that people who take melatonin may wake less often during the night and may find their sleep more refreshing.

Available in tablet form, the usual dose is from 1 to 3 milligrams (mg), taken up to an hour before bedtime. Use the synthetic form if available. Do not take melatonin during the day, as it may disrupt the body's sleep cycle.

*Caution:* Do not take melatonin if you have a family history of breast, endometrial, testicular, or prostate cancer; if you are pregnant or are trying to conceive; if you have an autoimmune disease, such as rheumatoid arthritis; or if you have cardiovascular disease.

## Valerian (Valeriana officinalis)

Known since Roman times, the dried roots of this perennial herb have long been used as a central nervous system sedative and treatment for insomnia. Valerian makes it easier to fall asleep and encourages deeper sleep cycles. The roots contain several essential oils that may be the source of the plant's sedating effect.

The root and rhizomes are sold in bulk for teas. Valerian may also be found at health food stores in capsule and tablet form (as a single herb or part of a formula); as a fluid extract; or as a tincture. The recommended dose is 300 to 500 milligrams, taken an hour before bedtime. Or you can mix one teaspoon of the tincture in a little warm water and drink it just before bed.

*Caution:* Because of its depressant effects, valerian should only be used for a short time. Also, avoid valerian if you're taking prescription sedatives, antidepressants, or mood-regulating medications.

## Kava kava

Another insomnia fighter, the root of this Australasian shrub is used to induce physical and mental relaxation. To prepare it as a tea, mix one tablespoon of the dried herb into 8 ounces of boiling water and let it steep for at least 30 minutes. Or you can take two 150-milligram capsules about 20 minutes before bedtime. (If you weigh more than 125 pounds, add another 75 milligrams of kava for each additional 30 pounds of body weight.)

*Caution:* Pregnant women, nursing mothers, or people who are clinically depressed shouldn't use kava. The herb can increase the potency of alcohol, barbiturates, and other drugs, although kava itself isn't addictive. Don't use it for more than three months without a physician's supervision.

## Other Flowers and Plants

Many other plants—such as Jamaican dogwood, lavender, lime blossom, lemon balm, Longan fruit, meadowsweet, hops, passionflower, skullcap, and vervain—are used in various forms to treat insomnia. Chamomile acts as a mild sedative and is often served as a calming tea. Lavender can be placed under your pillow (put it in a cheesecloth bag first) to promote a good night's sleep. Or treat yourself to a relaxing herbal bath before bed. Put two cups of fresh or dried herbs in a cloth bag and hang it from the faucet as you fill the tub with warm water.

## Tryptophan

One of the essential amino acids, tryptophan plays a key role in increasing serotonin, a neurotransmitter in the brain that affects sleep and mood. Tryptophan is found in all protein-rich foods (remember how sleepy you get after eating turkey on Thanksgiving?). It must be supplied by the diet as it cannot be produced by the body and is not available in supplement form (tryptophan supplements have been banned in the U.S. since 1989, when a contaminated batch was linked to several hundred cases of a serious blood disorder). Some good dietary sources of tryptophan include brown rice, cheese, poultry, and nuts.

# CHAPTER SIX

# Causes of Exhausted Nerves

## All the Stresses of Life

Magazines often list life problems according to their stress rating and ask you to add up your score—enough to invite a breakdown! It would have to be a very long list to include all the stressful events in life, so if your problem is not here don't feel it is unimportant. Anything that worries or hurts you is a stress. No matter how many people tell you it should not affect you, if it makes you feel stress, then it is on the list. Even a positive change can be stressful.

Because people feel guilty about being nervously ill, they often zero in on a list like this and say: "Yes, I have this, this, and this" . . . as if they need to justify being nervously strained. If your nerves are in trouble, then either you have pain in the present or you had it in the past; it is as simple as that.

Sometimes it is better not to look too hard for what caused the problem. You may become aware of the cause as your nerves heal.

# Some Life Stresses

- Death of a loved one
- Death of someone you felt you should have loved
- Divorce
- Loss of a relationship
- Physical illness
- Disability
- Loss of employment
- Stress at work
- Poverty
- Retirement
- Poor housing
- Getting old
- Growing up
- Being born
- Taking care of the elderly
- Taking care of the young
- Addictions
- Spiritual problems
- Taking care of the sick
- Exams (physical or academic)
- Promotion or job change
- Relatives or best friends moving away
- Getting married
- Having a baby
- Children leaving home
- Learning difficulties
- Moving
- Going on vacation
- Holidays
- Heavy physical work
- Long hours
- Poor working environment
- Working under deadlines
- Constant travel
- Too much responsibility (particularly in the young)
- The crying baby
- Being unhappy about your appearance
- Being worried about your sexuality
- Living in an unsafe neighborhood
- Fear of being raped or mugged
- Winning the lottery!

## The Past Affects Our Nerves—Stored Pain

We start storing pain early in life, certainly from birth, and probably from our days in the womb. The infant comes into the world with the need to be fed, loved, protected, and kept comfortable. If her needs are neglected and there is more pain (fear, anger, sadness, and so on) than she can cope with, then she tries to eliminate it by pushing it down into the "freezer" of her unconscious. This is the beginning of neurosis.

## Frozen Feelings—Neurosis

Neurosis is an illness of the feelings—a reaction to pain. This can occur at any stage of life. It starts when a person's "normal" reaction to stressful situations is to hide her real feelings. The happy child who feels safe and loved, and who is allowed to show her real feelings, has the confidence to be herself and let others see who she is. But an unhappy child, who must endure a difficult situation and try to make life bearable, tightens her body physically to hold in her emotions. This is called "armoring." She also manipulates her mind to react differently to unhappiness. This denial of real feelings leads to depression.

Here is an example: Jimmy sits quietly on the living room floor at the foster home, rocking back and forth. He does not cry; he speaks politely when spoken to. A casual observer might think he is well-mannered and content with his lot. But his behavior may really be saying, "I have tried screaming out in fear and rage because I am so unhappy. I still don't get what I need, so I tune out (become depressed). Since I cannot get away from the misery, I have to adapt to it."

## Children Want to Love Those Around Them

Children not only want to be loved, they are also very ready to love those around them. It is a great disappointment to them when they are treated as if their feelings don't matter. Being loved is not enough to develop identity. You have to be acknowledged as a thinking, feeling human being. That is not to say that you won't ever need guidance and discipline—you will; but if you are never able to express what you feel, you wilt inside.

## Learning to Role-Play

Susan is a little girl who loves her mother very much and is devoted to pleasing her. But most of the time, Susan's mother ignores her (remember, her mother may love her but still not see her needs). Susan is afraid, and thinks that if she is a good girl, life will be better. She is trying to trick her mind into believing she is happy playing the role of loving daughter. In reality, she is very angry and wants to say to her mother: "Why do you only think of your own worries? I am frightened and miserable too. You are grown up, I am only little."

## Carrying with Us the Fear of Losing Love

Susan is likely to carry on with this charade as she grows up. She is afraid, although perhaps not consciously, of finally losing her mother's love if she stops. It takes a great deal of energy to keep pretending things are fine and to push down the real feelings. But all the frustration and anger generated by the years of role-playing can leak out in neurotic behavior, which may be puzzling to both Susan and onlookers. Or it may burst out in nervous exhaustion (breakdown) when she is no longer able—or willing—to hold in the anger.

## The Path to Healing

The more a person has ignored his real emotions, the more likely he is to have a "drawer" in the unconscious labeled "not very nice feelings —keep this drawer shut." Fighting for space in the drawer would be bulging packages labeled rage, hate, jealousy, rejection, disappointment, and on and on.

We have seen that a hurt child freezes his real feelings in order to deal with his situation or to please his parents. Indeed, it may be the only possible reaction to the pain—and the best way to cope at the time. But as adults, we often continue to armor ourselves and put our real feelings in the freezer. Is it still appropriate to do this, or is it time to defrost the freezer and begin to heal?

## Defrost the Freezer

Have you ever emptied out the freezer to clean it, only to discover a dozen or more plastic containers pushed way to the back? Their unidentifiable contents look disgusting, and smell worse; the "use-by" dates are years old. You can't believe you've been wasting so much valuable freezer space and don't think twice about tossing everything into the garbage.

Now imagine you've been carrying the freezer and all of its contents around on your back all this time—only it's really in your unconscious. How much good is it doing you? How much energy does it require? Do you really need it? How much better would you feel if you didn't have to carry it with you everywhere you went?

It's time to let go of the old hurts and anger you've been carrying around and learn to show your real feelings.

## Learn to Love Yourself

People who are in pain need love and understanding. The sad and frightened child inside you is crying out for it. You can't change what happened to you in the past, but whatever age you are, it's not too late to start loving yourself. How can you have compassion for anyone else until you heal and nurture your own "inner child"? We are taught that it is selfish to think of ourselves. To think *only* of ourselves is selfish, but learning to love ourselves is an essential part of healing.

## Learn to Trust Yourself

It is so common for a nervously ill person to say: "I don't know who I am anymore." Is that surprising? We get into such a muddle trying to dodge our pain, please others (and occasionally ourselves—although we feel so guilty about it), and rely on other people's opinions to tell us who we are. You didn't have many choices when you were a child, but now you are an adult and it's time to start being yourself. No one else can live your life for you.

# CHAPTER SEVEN

# Learning to Be Yourself—Be Real

Our bodies want to be free from the armor of tension—they want to be real. Our minds want to be free too. Instead, we do a juggling act with our feelings to suit those around us—bending this way or that, first for parents, then for teachers, and still later for spouse or partner, children, boss, mother-in-law. When will it end? Only when you love yourself enough to be real.

This does not mean you have to stop loving the people who have played a part in your not being real, but it does means you owe it to yourself to acknowledge that you are a unique, important person, whatever your feelings are. It is your right to own your feelings; they are yours. It is between you and your conscience to decide whether your feelings are right or wrong.

No one can tell you how you *should* think or feel. There is no "should" about feelings—feelings just *are*. When you stop fighting yours and start to accept them, life not only gets simpler, it also gets much more exciting. You may not be proud of how you feel about some things, but at least you are listening to whom you really are. Change is possible when you have accepted what you want to change from.

It is important to encourage those around you, particularly young people, to own and express their feelings as well.

## Finding Your Own Answers

You may have to accept that no one is interested in your pain. There is nothing of medical significance wrong with you: you don't have a raised white cell count, an abnormal brain scan, or any interesting delusions that could cause a professional to say, "Aha, just as I thought—a classic case!" It's just you, lonely in the middle of a family, struggling to keep going, one gray day after another, puzzled that you feel guilty about sitting in your apartment, having everything that money could buy, surrounded by dirty coffee cups and cigarette butts, with stains on your clothes.

## You Have a Choice

The following choices are available to you, but only you can make them. Are you willing to:

- Take responsibility for your physical and emotional health?

- Look at the part you are playing in your own unhappiness?

- Stop hurting yourself with alcohol, drugs, cigarettes, poor food, lack of sunshine, and no exercise?

- Stop feeling sorry for yourself?

- Find out what your real needs are?

- Stop trying to please people all the time?

- Accept that you can't change the people around you—you can only stop their attitudes hurting you?

- Accept that if you don't take care of yourself, you can be a terrible burden on those around you?

- Accept that you are causing a lot of your anxiety and depression by the way you think of yourself?

- Be *yourself*—not what those around you think you should be?

## Learning to Be Yourself—Assertion

This can be very liberating and need not be accomplished by bulldozing through your relationships with anger, saying: "Look out, the real me is coming; I'm not going to be pushed around any longer!" It can be done gently, and with love—but be prepared for criticism, no matter how you tackle it.

## Why Are Relationships Such Hard Work?

Would relationships be such a strain if we accepted people the way they are and let them see us the way we are, warts and all? We have seen that real feelings produce healthy behavior: a balanced outlook, ability to adjust to change, ability to cope. Suppressed feelings produce neurotic behavior, anxiety, and depression. As you start to be honest with yourself, being honest with those around you is the next step. Don't forget, of course, that you cannot expect *other* people to change: you can only show them how their behavior affects you.

## Open, Honest Communication

Imagine the following scene:

*Place:* John's Bar, the venue for the weekly meeting of Bill, Tony, and George. They have been friends for years. The time is early April. Each week they talk about sports, the office, and, according to the season, crabgrass, aphids, their summer vacations, or the difference double window panes makes to their heating bills. It's a bit early for baseball and the aphids are not yet in evidence; tonight they are going to talk about feelings (at least George is).

Bill and Tony are at the bar when George comes in. They exchange greetings. Then Bill notices that George's eyes look red.

*Bill:* Hay fever already, buddy?

*George:* (Rather sheepishly) No, actually, I've just had a few tears.

*Bill and Tony:* Tears! (They could not have been more embarrassed if George had just said he had wet himself.)

*Bill:* (Gravely) Geez, there's nothing wrong with Betty, is there, George?

*George:* (Smiling) No, Betty's fine, everything's fine.

*Tony:* (His curiosity overcoming his embarrassment) Well, what were you crying about?

*George:* I wasn't really crying. Life felt so good; I was in the garden before I came out, the sun was still warm, a blackbird was picking moss from the gutter for its nest, and I could hear Betty playing an old song on the piano—I felt moved—tears came, so I let them. That's all it was. They told me that I had to let my feelings out when I had that little heart attack last year.

*Bill and Tony:* (Together, after a stunned silence) Who's for another round, then?

For the next hour they talk about the rust on Bill's car, the current government screw-ups, and the latest computer gizmos. George, looking happy and relaxed, makes his way to the bathroom. Tony's and Bill's eyes meet over their beer glasses.

*Bill:* Do you think he's all right?

*Tony:* I don't know, but I do know he had a cousin in Pittsburgh who went a little crazy.

These men's lives are ruled by hiding their fears and sadness even from those close to them.

Bill is afraid of flying, of his wife dying before him, of being laid off. He is sad about his father getting old, and he still grieves for his dog. He keeps his feelings to himself.

Tony slept with the light on until he was married. His wife has no idea he is still very uneasy in the dark. She wishes he would be as organized about other things as he is about impending power blackouts—boxes of candles and flashlights are all over the place. He feels full of sadness and compassion about a neighbor's handicapped child, although he completely ignores the boy and avoids the parents if he can. He worries about his smoking but gets angry if it is mentioned. He loves his wife dearly, but rarely tells her so.

George has felt very guilty for years because he knew he had hurt his wife deeply by not wanting to see their stillborn son. He was gripped with a fear that he could not understand at the thought of seeing the dead baby. Some months after the birth, he was dozing in front of the fire after a bout of the flu and dreamed about a baby brother who had died at birth. George had been four at the time. He felt distressed when he woke up and remembered how afraid he felt when he had been made to kiss the waxen little cheek. He also remembered being sent to an aunt and how she hurt him when she scrubbed his face. The dream gave him some insight into his guilt, but he still could not bring himself to share it with his wife. When he did tell her years later (he had just come out of the hospital), they both had a good cry—and all his wife's hurt about George's apparent indifference to their loss disappeared.

## What Will Others Think?

If you do not show your real feelings to those around you, aren't you continuing with the mistakes started by the adults in your young life? When we are little, we think: "When I am grown up, I will do this, this, and this," but *do* we? Or do we just carry on hiding our feelings and play-acting to make sure people won't dislike us or, worse still, walk away and leave us? We go on saying "yes" when we mean "no," and "no" when we mean "yes"—but at what cost?

# CHAPTER EIGHT

# Understanding the Nature of Anxiety

When we come to understand the nature of anxiety, we can make it dissolve. There are three main types of anxiety: outside anxiety, inside anxiety, and "judge and jury" anxiety. What they all have in common are the physical symptoms. The causes may differ, though the effect on the body is the same.

One young man wept during his first lesson on how to cope with anxiety. His tears were a mixture of relief and anger; years of pills and much misery could have been avoided if he had understood what was happening.

## Outside Anxiety

This is worry about real threats to the body or life circumstances; for example, having an operation or losing a job. Sometimes the threat is so frightening that the sufferer resists facing the source of his fears, and turns them into physical symptoms. He denies having any life problems and becomes evasive when the doctor asks if he has any worries. His denial is not an untruth; it is the truth as he sees it.

## Inside Anxiety

Here the fear comes from within and is caused by thoughts. Not thoughts like "What will happen if I don't pass my final exams," as in outside anxiety, but vague inner fears that the sufferer may only half recognize, such as fear of losing control, of punishment, of being unlovable, of destructive feelings (perhaps toward family members). Sufferers often have an overwhelming fear of reprisal; for example, hating the boss but not daring to show it. This can lead to self-hatred, or to what is seen as cowardice.

## "Judge and Jury" Anxiety

The moral teaching we receive as children is often another source of anxiety—worry about guilt. As we grow up, we continue to listen to the old tapes in our head and develop an internal "judge and jury" system far more severe than our original teachings. Here there is a mix of anticipatory guilt: being terrified of doing anything that would be condemned by society, and feeling a deep sense of frustration at having to go through the same, stupid routines in order to keep our anxieties at bay. Here, for example, would be the man who always says "Yes" because he can't stand the feelings of guilt when he says "No." He finds it very restricting to have to drive his mother 15 miles to her friend's house to play bridge each Sunday, but would rather do this than face the guilt. He is his own judge *and* his own hanging jury.

### Consider What Disapproval Means to You

How do I feel when someone disapproves of me? Anxious/trapped/hurt/depressed/like a naughty child? Do I take actions to avoid disapproval, even over small things, and then hate myself for being weak? Do I do this over and over again?

### The Effects of This "Judge and Jury" System

When, as children, we are constantly bombarded with: "You must be a good child, consider the feelings of others..." what we are really hearing is: "Beat yourself with sticks, turn yourself inside out, do whatever is necessary to achieve, strive to appear socially acceptable, and always put the feelings of others first." There is something very wrong here. Surely, we need to be taught to love others as ourselves and give our feelings equal consideration. A system that teaches us to ignore our own needs runs the risk of producing either self-effacing martyrs, or people who rebel, think only of themselves, and take pleasure in riding roughshod over the feelings of others.

## Guilt

If the judge and members of the jury are placed on their bench and in the jury chairs during childhood, the prisoner is never acquitted but is out on probation forever, living in fear of committing a "crime" against society, because the thought of the punishment (guilt) is so distressing.

Some people are so worried about guilt, they are permanently tense. Could this be the cause of many obsessions and phobias?

## Free-floating Anxiety

Where there is no obvious cause for the fear, it is called free-floating—not attached to anything.

The perplexed person will say: "I have absolutely nothing to be anxious about, yet I am in a state of fear all the time." It is unlikely that his subconscious would agree with him. It is more likely to be poking him to get rid of old fears, which he is trying to hold down with his intellect: "I am financially secure, my wife loves me," and the like. This rationalizing does not work. You cannot dupe the subconscious—it has a record of the truth.

## Ghosting

Carlos' way of coping with past pain was: "If you don't think about it, it will go away." That might work for a while, but invariably a trigger from the present can bring the old feelings to life again and they nag away at you. This is called "ghosting"—the unhooking of emotions of long ago from the unconscious. This is how it happened to Carlos, although it does not need to be as dramatic as this. The next time you react to something with more anger or sadness than the situation deserves, ask yourself about the feelings. Is there more anger in you than you would like to admit? Is a sad thought enough to push you into depression because you hover on the edge of it all the time? Is there something from your past that you never really came to terms with?

Carlos' only daughter was going off to work in Canada, and he could not understand his strong reaction against this. He began to feel anxious and depressed and had a terrible sense of loss. It did not even make sense. He knew he would see her several times a year and, even more puzzling, he knew he was delighted she had the opportunity to live in another country and get to know its people.

## Throwing Out Old Feelings

After several talk-therapy sessions, Carlos' feelings that he had kept bottled up for years came pouring out.

Most of his childhood had been miserable. His mother left the family home when he was 13, and he feared his father's temper so much that he had to work very hard to keep things running smoothly. This involved taking more than his share of responsibility for a younger sister. His father saw Carlos as a sensible, caring boy. He did not see that he was also full of anger and fear.

At first Carlos was very embarrassed about crying over something that had happened so long ago, but saw how the old fear of loss had been affecting his present feelings. He was rather hard to live with as his anger surfaced, but his family was supportive. He made good progress in therapy and said he felt physically lighter, as though a weight had been lifted off him. He had laid his "ghost" to rest.

# CHAPTER NINE

# Understanding the Nature of Depression

Depression is very different from just being unhappy. When we are unhappy, we can acknowledge the sadness about something in our lives, or in the lives of people close to us, but gradually the feeling affects us less and less, and we are able to be comforted and live normally in spite of a heavy heart.

In depression, this is not so. Sufferers are unable to adjust to the painful feelings, so they switch them off and become emotionally dead. Unfortunately, the good feelings that would balance their moods are also turned off, so it is difficult or impossible to comfort them.

It is sad that many people go through years of being only half alive, not realizing they are suffering from a treatable illness. If your finger became numb and you could not use it, you would be rushing off to the doctor to find the cause of the trouble. Why put up with numb feelings? Depression is often so sneaky; it creeps up on you, anesthetizing your feelings little by little until your lack of emotions hardly registers and you accept your gray world as normal.

One young woman said: "Being depressed is like being in a room that needs decorating—but you don't know it needs decorating, so you can't do anything about it. All you know is a sense of dull misery and bewilderment that you have to stay in such a room."

When she realized she was suffering from depression, she said it was like being able to see the cracks on the wall. She felt the insight was optimistic, and she now knew why she had been in the gray room, but it also brought its problems: how could she make it a better room to live in? It can be even more painful at first when the feelings start to wake up and, inevitably, anxieties rear their heads—how will I plaster the walls, will I ever find the right paint? and so on.

Though scary, it can also be very exciting—because the good feelings are going to come through too. This is the start of recovery.

A young man described it like this: "It was as though I had undergone surgery and been under an anesthetic for years—as I began to come out of the depression, my wound started to throb, but at least I was now awake enough to believe people when they were saying the throbbing would eventually go away and I would be myself again."

## Who Is Likely to Suffer from Depression?

Anyone and everyone can suffer from depression—although hereditary factors do come into play in some types of depression.

## Terms Used for Depression (Rightly or Wrongly)

All the following are used by people when they talk about their own or others' depression; the terms are not precise synonyms.

Mood disorder, affective disorder, reactive depression, endogenous depression, neurotic depression, bipolar disorder, manic depression, psychotic depression, retarded depression, agitated depression, dysthymic disorder, personality disorder, dependent personality, masked depression.

Since this book deals with mild to moderate states of anxiety and depression, psychotic depression will not be discussed because it is part of a more severe illness that definitely needs professional help.

# Types of Depression

For our purposes it will be enough to look initially at three types of depression: outside depression, inside depression, and mixed depression.

## Outside Depression

Sometimes called exogenous, reactive, or neurotic depression, this term means reacting to life circumstances with depression. When the change in the person's life is sad—for example, bereavement, divorce, loss of employment—it is easy to see why there would be an alteration in mood. Sometimes, however, people can become depressed about very minor life changes that would not affect other people.

There can be many reasons for this. They can have a backlog of events that have not been dealt with. They may not have had time to get over one blow, however small, before the next one lands. Or they may habitually react with depression because they were taught to respond in this way. In the same way that you can teach a child to be anxious, you can also teach him or her to be depressed.

## Inside Depression

This is also called endogenous depression—coming from within. Some professionals say this type of depression is caused by a fault in the body chemistry, and the reason for this is unknown. But things do not go wrong in the body or mind without a reason. There may not be an obvious reason in the present life circumstances: "What has *she* got to be depressed about? She loves her husband and children, is a full partner in the firm, and drives a Porsche." But there will certainly be a reason in the past.

Before you say: "Ah, yes, but that was a long time ago and she has had an easy time since then," remember that if past hurtful feelings are not expressed, they do not obligingly go away. They can leap out at you when you least expect it and force you to settle old scores. The pushed-down feelings that are most likely to cause depression later are anger, frustration, sadness, guilt, and, of course, the real killer: low self-esteem —feeling unattractive or worthless. It is vital to realize that the reality of the situation does not matter; it is the feelings that are important. For example, an unattractive man who has spent his life working on a road-maintenance crew may never have experienced depression—he could feel very good about himself. However, a man who looked like, say, Tom Cruise, and had Cruise's bank balance, could be very depressed. No matter how successful you may be in the present, or how many people tell you what a wonderful person you are, if you suffer from low self-esteem and are pushing around a wheelbarrow full of negative feelings about yourself, you are going to stay depressed. Tip those feelings onto the compost pile—express them—and you will recover.

## Mixed Depressions

Many people have a mixture of outside and inside depression—difficult life circumstances, plus a reduced ability to cope because of neurosis.

### AGITATED DEPRESSION

Normally, depression is associated with slowing down, but in this type of depression the person is also very restless and anxious. He can't win —he can't even have the rest that depression usually brings.

### SMILING DEPRESSION

Some people go to great lengths to hide being "down" or "blue." Think of the joke-a-minute person you know who uses humor as a mechanism to hold in his pain and fool others. Perhaps it could be called the "clown" syndrome: smiling mouth and sad eyes.

### MASKED DEPRESSION

Here the symptoms take a physical form—backache, headaches, digestive upsets. Sufferers may not be aware of the causes of their troubles and even deny they are depressed.

### MANIC DEPRESSION

Self-help can be recommended only for the milder forms of this illness. Self-help can, however, be used effectively along with medical treatment. Taking care can help prevent recurrences. Manic depression (also known as bipolar disorder) is when the mood swings from very low to very high spirits. Some people with mania enjoy their "highs," but many find them just as upsetting as the lows—because they know that their personality changes. It can be particularly distressing for relatives, who must clean up after them. Sufferers' thoughts and actions are so speeded up that they can work faster, be creative, and often achieve a great deal—though they can also be reckless about driving, spending money, and making big decisions. They can have the same attitude to relationships—off with the old, on with the new. If you see a friend behaving out of character, suggest that her nerves are exhausted and encourage her to seek help. It may be quite a task; she may have an inflated opinion of herself and think life is great—but it won't last long. The nervous system cannot cope—what goes too far up has to come a long way down. The crash will come. And it may be a rude awakening to discover that what seemed like productivity was actually just "wheel spinning."

## Seasonal Affective Disorder (SAD)

SAD, or the "winter blues," is a recurrent depression some people suffer that starts about the same time every year. When the amount of daylight diminishes in early autumn, especially in northern climes, sufferers experience symptoms that grow worse as the days shorten.

It usually starts by increased need for sleep and reduced concentration and progresses to depression, anxiety, irritability, and loss of sexual interest. Other signs are aches and pains, and cravings for sweet foods and bread.

As spring approaches, the symptoms improve, and usually by about May sufferers recover and resume a normal life. For some, unfortunately, even though they feel better, the disruption caused by the illness year after year leads them into "ordinary" depression, because it becomes impossible to pick up the pieces of their lives each spring. Studies are interrupted, jobs lost, relationships ruined.

Happily, once the nature of the depression is recognized, the illness can be avoided. It is not a new condition but a newly discovered one.

Recent research is very exciting. The cure is to be out more in daylight, or, for severe sufferers, to be exposed to special lights (full-spectrum lighting). The pineal gland is stimulated by light, and this keeps one's hormones balanced and prevents the problem.

For mild SAD symptoms, spending 20 to 30 minutes outdoors (without sunglasses) in the brightest part of the day or working near an open window may be enough. If the symptoms are severe, the installation of full-spectrum lighting in the home may be necessary. These lights can be ordered by mail from various distributors (see the Referral List on page 133). Also, many major hardware and lighting stores now carry them in response to the increased demand as people become more aware of the problem. Low-dose melatonin supplementation may also be useful (see page 28).

## What Does Depression Feel Like?

Here are some descriptive comments made by sufferers:

* I have no interest in anything or anyone; I know I still love my family but I can't feel it.

* I feel exhausted; my thoughts are slow and even talking is an effort. I struggle to get the kids off to school, and then just sit at the breakfast table and stare at the wall until lunchtime.

* I feel so worthless and guilty.

* Time seems to stand still.

* There seems to be a gray mist over everything—I just want to stay in bed and pull the blanket over my head.

* I can't bear to watch television in case I see something sad— I can't stop crying.

* It's such an effort to be with people—nobody understands. I have to pretend to be normal; it's sheer agony.

* All the things I did cheerfully now seem like impossible tasks—even making a meal or watering the plants.

* I used to love clothes and make-up; but some days I don't even wash or get out of my pajamas.

- I look at people and feel bewildered by their interest in things: reading, playing golf, painting—I think, why do they bother? Everything seems pointless.

- I feel like I'm such a burden to my family; would they be better off without me?

- If only I could sleep; I wake between four and five times each night, and then toss and turn.

- If only I could get off to sleep; it is often three o'clock before I drop off, and then I can't rouse myself in the morning.

- If only I could cry; the tears are inside but I can't get them out.

- I worry all the time about the future; it looks so bleak.

- I have absolutely no interest in eating. Food doesn't have any taste to it.

- Have I been so bad? Is this a punishment?

- I feel as if there's a weight in my stomach.

- My chest feels heavy; I keep sighing.

- I keep thinking I have heart trouble or cancer; I can't stop talking about it.

- I will do anything to avoid sex.

- I can struggle through the day but the feeling gets worse toward evening.

Be encouraged by the feelings of others. You are not alone, you are not going 'round the bend, and you will recover. Other people do; so can you!

## Glimpses of Getting Better

It can be slow at first. Here are some comments:

- I looked at Ben in his crib and for a few seconds I could actually feel my love for him; it was such a relief. I know my feelings for my baby will come back now.

• I woke up and thought: "I'll have some coffee and go out for a newspaper." I hadn't thought about a paper for months. I usually think, "Oh God, how will I get through the day?" It didn't last, but it gave me hope.

• I used to always be ready with a negative answer when someone tried to encourage me, but now I've stopped doing this.

• I had to force myself to go to Teresa's school play—and was surprised how well I coped with the crowd and the noise.

• My wife was angry; I went into the garage to escape. When I went back in the house I was amazed; two hours had passed. I had straightened up the work bench and potted some bulbs. Apart from pushing myself to the office, it was the first time I had gotten out of the recliner for weeks.

• It was the first time in years that I hadn't died inside when Nick mentioned a vacation. We might even let a little romance blossom.

• Food has begun to have taste again, and I actually bought a magazine the other day.

• I don't argue with John so much. I am shocked at how selfish I have been; so wrapped up in myself I didn't give him a thought. Now we talk more.

• It took me a long time to accept that it was depression, but when I did, I started to go forward.

• I feel as if a curtain has been lifted. I am having more and more good days, although when I am having a bad day it's hard to remember the good ones.

• It was a small thing but I still remember it: the color of the grass registered. It was a lovely green and I could see it. It was like coming out of prison.

# CHAPTER TEN

# What Is a Nervous Breakdown?

This generally means having anxiety and/or depression to a degree where a normal life is not possible.

Psychiatrists spend a lot of time discussing the difference between anxiety and depression. It must be difficult for the family doctor or HMO (health maintenance organization) physician to make the distinction in a six-minute consultation. Sometimes it is clearly more one than the other, but very often the nervously exhausted person is suffering from a mixture of the two. It can happen that as the anxiety feelings ease, the depression starts, or vice versa.

The common and much-feared term "nervous breakdown" mistakenly conjures up an image of someone being transported to a psychiatric ward in a straitjacket. Claire Weekes, in her books, very wisely uses the words "sensitized nerves" instead of nervous breakdown. Before using other terms, perhaps this bogeyman could be laid to rest once and for all; these are only *words*. If someone is told they are having a breakdown, they are understandably afraid. If they are told their nerves are exhausted or oversensitized, it means the same thing, but it does not alarm them as much. We all have nervous breakdowns regularly—it's only a matter of degree. If our nervous systems cannot cope with repeated stresses, reactions like "blowing your top" or "losing your cool" result. These could be seen as minibreakdowns. If the nervous system does not "hold up," then it must break down! A major breakdown can be said to be a major reaction to a major degree of stress (pain).

## Do People Recover from Nervous Breakdowns?

Of course—broken-down nervous systems can be built up again. Some years ago the British National Association for Mental Health produced a poster showing a healthy, pretty young girl saying: "I have forgotten my nervous breakdown, but my friends haven't." What it expresses is a sad reflection on our attitude to nervous illness. It is easy to forget a person's gallbladder operation or broken hip, but a nervous breakdown is quite a different matter. The memory of the changed behavior—mood swings, irritability, suspiciousness—often lingers, and doubts about whether this is the normal personality remain: "Will it happen again?" is the unspoken thought. Happily, the person who has recovered from a breakdown is often more stable than her friends who are ignoring the state of their nerves.

A breakdown can have the effect of a giant spring-cleaning of the unconscious—the floodgates are open, the person has lost his armor and is too weak to hold back his pain any longer. The tremendous energy involved in the long-term suppression of feelings is discharged, leaving the person tired, but in a state where it is possible to heal.

## Treatments for Nervous Breakdowns

We humans have always looked for a substance to help us cope with fear. We have found many that temporarily relieve our symptoms—but at what cost? A deterioration in our physical health (we cannot swallow poisons daily and expect to keep healthy), and the inevitable change in personality that comes from long-term sedation or stimulation of the nervous system. There is also the problem of our growing dependence on drugs. And medication may numb you to the point that you are never able to work out the pain (you've just pushed it down) or take the steps needed to truly heal.

At the moment, self-help groups and services all around the United States are endeavoring to clean up a decades-long mess caused by the overuse of tranquilizers and sleeping pills (see Chapter Eleven).

## Going to the Doctor with Nerves

Many patients reveal only a few of their symptoms to the doctor. They are too embarrassed to recount what seems to be a long list of unrelated problems, and often hesitate to ask questions.

### *An Ideal Consultation*

Sick people need to understand what is making them ill:

"Your tests are negative; you don't need drugs or surgery, but you do need help," the doctor might say. "Because you have had so much stress, your body is producing too much adrenaline and that is the cause of those strange feelings. You are going to have to learn to slow down. There is a class here on Tuesdays at 7:30 P.M.

"If you feel desperate for a rest," the doctor continues, "I could give you tranquilizers for up to two weeks, but it would be better if you could manage without them. It's not safe to give these drugs for long periods, because you could become addicted to them and they can cause depression. The other problem with them is that you cannot adjust to your problems if you suppress them with sedatives. It's like splinting an injured arm: useful for a short time, but the arm will not regain full strength until the splint is removed.

"I'll tell the counselor you are coming to the class. Do you promise to come back and see me if you don't feel you are making progress?"

After a consultation of this type, the patient leaves feeling that his misery has been acknowledged, and he has had some explanation, however brief, about the cause of his symptoms. He knows there will be ongoing support.

Unfortunately, it is not an ideal world and few doctors and fewer health maintenance organizations will offer referrals to a counselor or relaxation therapist. Happily, there are doctors who are moving away from the prescription pad, and who realize the value of education and support. Many arrange longer consultations, and provide their patients with referrals to yoga and meditation classes, as well as written information on anxiety and depression.

## An Unsatisfactory Consultation

What the doctor may think of as an optimistic, reassuring consultation:

"All your tests are negative; it's all nerves, just go home and forget about it," the doctor says, and ends the visit. This usually leaves the patient feeling miserable and confused. The symptoms are still there, and she has no idea how to get rid of them. She may have longed for a test to reveal the cause of her misery. What she needs to know is that there *is* a cause, although it may not be the hoped-for low thyroid levels, anemia, or hernia that could be cured with a magic pill or surgery.

She leaves the clinic knowing she should feel relieved about the tests, but finds it hard to accept that so many symptoms can be caused by nerves. Is it her fault? If there is no reason for the symptoms and no treatment, then she must be *imagining* she is feeling so awful. She may already be aware of the reactions of those around her to people with "nerves" and may fabricate a story rather than face the humiliation of telling family and friends.

## The Doctor Has Nerves Too

There is no excuse for a doctor's being indifferent to your emotional pain, routinely handing out lethal pharmacological cocktails, or abruptly stopping your tranquilizers. However, if you consider what her life involves, it might dissipate some of your anger toward her. How many times have you shouted at someone: "I can't do everything!"? When you think of it, that is just what a doctor is expected to do. Everything from prescribing the right medication for each patient's ailment to knowing a diagnosis of every known disease. She also has to cope with some very difficult situations. For instance, she has to know how to get through a consultation with a violent patient, or take the anger of grieving relatives. She is being inundated with paperwork from bureaucratic insurance companies and second-guessed by claims adjusters with no medical background. Don't forget that she is a human being too, and has only the limits of her own personality to work in. She could be anxious and depressed as well. (There was a report a few years ago suggesting that the higher the doctor's anxiety levels were, the more likely he was to prescribe tranquilizers for his patients.)

Doctors are often not very good at assessing the emotional states of their patients: this may be because not enough time is given to this during their training, or it may be due to their own embarrassment or fear. They are not robots trained simply to label disease and to excise cysts. Having to deal with the emotions of others must at times be like rubbing salt into their own wounds. A white coat does not make them immune. Imagine what it must be like to have three recently bereaved people in one hospital when your own wife is terminally ill. Who supports the doctor? It is a pity that the fear of being perceived as "non-professional" does not allow doctors to share what they are feeling. Our hurts are a great leveler—the one thing we all have in common.

## Why Is Nervous Illness So Misunderstood?

Because there is nothing dramatic to be seen, the sufferer is often treated like a hypochondriac or malingerer. It is easy to understand a fever in someone with pneumonia, or why there is pain in a broken limb, but it is often much harder to accept that nervously ill people have disabling symptoms too. If the person who is obviously physically ill or injured becomes irritable or depressed, this is seen as part of the illness and treated with concern. But people with nervous troubles often get little sympathy unless they become seriously ill and need in-patient care.

## How Do We Know When Our Nerves Are in Danger?

The early warnings sent out by the nervous system are quite vague and often ignored. Symptoms include: losing energy, feeling irritable, experiencing a change in eating or sleeping habits, and generally losing interest in life. If you don't slow down, the nervous system gives up and lets chaos reign—hence all the symptoms.

The person who says, "This came on suddenly, I was fine last week," has really not noticed how strained his nerves have become. They are now forcing him to stop and take notice. How useful it would be if, from our infancy, every time we pushed our nerves too far we broke out in a rash of green spots. We would then be aware of the damage we were doing—and could slow down until the spots disappeared.

# CHAPTER ELEVEN

# Drug and Nondrug Treatments for Depression and Anxiety

## Drug Treatment for Anxiety

There was a time in the 1970s when the tranquilizer Valium (diazepam) was the most widely prescribed drug in the United States—more than 30 million prescriptions were written each year. A completely new type of medication created originally to treat anxiety, Valium and Librium (chlordiazepoxide)—and others like them—were hailed as wonder drugs that could treat a variety of ills. They were supposed to be safe and nonaddictive, with minimal side effects. Unfortunately, researchers were only beginning to understand the complex workings of the brain, and the promises weren't to prove true. Since then, research has continued and newer and more effective antidepressants and sleep medications are now being prescribed. These will be discussed on the following pages.

## SSRI Antidepressants—generic (and trade) names

Citalopram (Cipramil)

Fluoxetine (Prozac)

Fluvoxamine (Luvox)

Paroxetine (Paxil)

Sertraline (Lustral, Zoloft)

## Tricyclic Antidepressants—generic (and trade) names

Amitriptyline (Elavil, Endep, Tryptanol)

Amoxapine (Asendin)

Clomipramine (Anafranil)

Desipramine (Norpramin, Pertofran)

Doxepin (Adapin, Sinequan)

Imipramine (Janimine, Tofranil)

Maprotiline (Ludiomil)

Nortriptyline (Aventyl, Pamelor)

Protriptyline (Concordin, Triptil, Vivactil)

Trazodone (Desyrel, Molipaxin)

Trimiparine (Surmontil)

## "Novel" Antidepressants—generic (and trade) names

Bupropion (Wellbutrin)

Nefazadone (Serzone)

Venlafaxine (Effexor)

## There Is No Need to Panic

If you are taking the drugs mentioned below, please note:

1. You may not be dependent on them.

2. If you are dependent, by a careful reduction plan and looking after yourself, you can make a full recovery.

3. How do you know if you are dependent? If you feel the pills are no longer working the way they did, and you have to increase the dose to get the same effect, or if you feel ill when you stop taking them—then you could be dependent.

4. Consult your doctor and read *Free Yourself from Tranquilizers and Sleeping Pills* (see Further Reading and Reference, page 125). It offers a complete guide to withdrawal.

Doctors these days are much more informed about withdrawal than they once were, but in case you need information see the appendix.

## Drug Treatment for Depression

If you are severely depressed, you *must* see your doctor. He will probably prescribe antidepressant drugs. For some people, these can be very effective and may dramatically improve the quality of their lives. It is unwise, however, to use them for mild or moderate depression. A great many people recover completely with self-help methods or with no treatment at all. (Note that placebos have been 20 percent to 40 percent effective in many antidepressant drug studies!) And antidepressants, like many other drugs, can have unpleasant side effects such as drowsiness, heartburn, weight gain, headaches, confusion, panic, dry mouth, constipation, and sexual problems.

Many different types of antidepressants are now available. They all have similar goals: to increase the levels of certain key chemicals in the brain, thus improving mood. Some have very good results but others, because of their side effects, are very unsatisfactory. The two types of drugs most commonly prescribed are the SSRIs (Selective Serotonin Reuptake Inhibitors)—Prozac and Zoloft are examples—and the tricyclic antidepressants (tricyclic refers to the drug's chemical structure) such as To-franil and Elavil. The so-called "novel" antidepressants such as Ser-zone and Wellbutrin are neither SSRI nor tricyclic, but have similar effects. Another group of antidepressant drugs, the MAOIs (monoamine oxidase inhibitors), are less commonly used, as they can have serious interactions with certain foods and strict dietary restrictions must be followed. Lithium and drugs called the phenothiazines are used to se-date manic episodes.

## How Antidepressant Drugs Work

In our brains, there are chemicals called neurotransmitters; the level of these neurotransmitters affects our mood. More than 50 neurotransmitters have been identified thus far, with many more expected as research into the chemistry of the brain advances.

In depression, fewer neurotransmitters are released. Antidepressant drugs act to raise the levels of neurotransmitters in the brain.

Some antidepressants (for example, amitriptyline) are mainly sedative and would be prescribed for someone who is both anxious and de-pressed. Others (for example, imipramine) lack this calming effect, and are given to people who are lethargic.

## The SSRI Antidepressants

These drugs are popular because they do not produce the side effects of dry mouth, weight gain, and oversedation associated with the tri-cyclics. However, they do have their own characteristic side effects, which can include nausea, vomiting, agitation, impaired sexual func-tion, and even suicidal feelings.

Special mention is made of Prozac because it is the best known of the SSRIs, having replaced Valium as the "wonder drug" of choice (in 1990, it even appeared on the cover of *Newsweek*!). Controversy continues as to whether Prozac is a miracle cure for depression or a dangerous drug responsible for the suicidal feelings and actions of large numbers of people.

It would seem that both these points are valid: many doctors have found it to be a miracle for some and a nightmare for others (Zoloft is now the most commonly prescribed of the SSRIs). Here are two typical experiences with Prozac:

• *Woman aged 49:* I had lived for 15 years with the nightmare of depression. Not a day passed without my considering taking my life. I had been given many types of antidepressants, but they made little difference. However, after about ten days on Prozac I found it easier to work and I had more energy. I did not dare to hope it would continue, but it did—and I improved more and more.

My friends have said I seem on a permanent "high." I am aware of this and of how much I talk, but I don't care. I feel happy, and am able to enjoy my work and traveling. I intend to stay on Prozac for the rest of my life.

• *Woman aged 38:* I had suffered several periods of depression in my life and had always just worked through them. Last year I was feeling low again and my doctor suggested Prozac. The first day I took them my digestion was upset, but I thought this was only to be expected. The next day I began to feel very agitated (much more than I had been), and by day five I was in a terrible state. I was overwhelmed by suicidal feelings that I had never had before and could not sleep or eat. My family was very worried and called the doctor. She said the pills would take up to two weeks before they were really effective and urged me to continue taking them. She did not seem to associate my suicidal feelings with the drug, and said that these feelings were a common symptom in depression. I tried to tell her that I had never had these feelings before, and that I was no stranger to depression. On day ten I decided the cure was much worse than the complaint, so I stopped the pills. What a relief; I felt weepy and "down," but the awful agitation, nausea, and suicidal feelings disappeared as quickly as they came. I went back to the doctor, whose attitude was, "If you don't take the medication, how can you expect to get better?" I felt hurt and frustrated because she would not believe that the pills had made me so much worse. I really felt at risk. I wonder how many patients they lose like that!

## The MAOI Antidepressants

MAOIs allow the neurotransmitters to increase, thus producing stimulation in the brain. These particular drugs work by blocking the action of one of the brain enzymes. As a result of this action, certain foods and drugs cannot be taken during MAOI therapy because of the risk of a rise in blood pressure. If you have headaches or experience nausea while taking MAOIs, then see your doctor immediately. Patients on these drugs are always given a card listing prohibited drugs and food. The foods concerned are tyramine-rich foods such as cheese, yeast, red wine, meat extracts (meat stock cubes), and fava beans.

Even after discontinuation of MAOIs, the drugs stay in the bloodstream for at least two weeks. It is therefore essential to continue avoiding the relevant foods and drugs during this time. If your doctor asks you to take another drug before this two weeks is up, it would be wise to question it.

## Withdrawal from Antidepressants

It took the majority of the members of the medical profession many years to accept that withdrawal from antidepressants and sleeping pills such as Halcion (triazolam), even after small therapeutic doses, could cause a dramatic (and, in many instances, protracted) illness in a large number of users. In spite of the information (although it is agreed that it is understated, often for reasons of legal liability) in the pharmacological handbooks, and information gleaned from case histories in medical journals highlighting symptoms caused by withdrawal from antidepressants, the problems concerning withdrawal are still very often overlooked. **Any drug that sedates or stimulates is potentially a drug of dependence.**

### Withdraw from Antidepressants Slowly

• *Man aged 30:* I have taken Prozac twice—for about six months each time. The first time it really lifted me and motivated me to look for work and take more interest in the home. I was doing well, so I decided to stop taking it. I now know it was foolish, but I just stopped it overnight. After a couple of days I began to feel ill; my muscles and joints ached, and I felt very down and confused. My doctor said it was nothing to do with stopping Prozac and I must have a bug. It took me about four weeks to pull up from this and I coped for about nine months until I began to feel depressed again. It was my wife who suggested I should go back on Prozac. The doctor was quite happy about this suggestion and it was just like the first time: it bucked me up in no time, and after about six months I felt I no longer needed it. I stopped it while on vacation and had exactly the same experience as the first time, but this time I knew it was definitely withdrawal from Prozac I was feeling. There was no mistaking how my muscles felt and what state of mind I was in. I had no wish to argue with the doctor, so I continued on the full dose until I felt better (the symptoms vanished after a couple of doses), and then I cut down gradually.

## The Dos and Don'ts of Taking Antidepressants

1. Do be patient; the drugs will not work overnight. It can take several weeks to see an effect on mood.

2. Beware of too many repeat prescriptions; see your doctor if you develop a rash, experience severe side effects, or if you've been on your medication for a while and start to feel "high" or "manic."

3. When it is time to withdraw, do it gradually. People coming off antidepressants may experience withdrawal symptoms. Such symptoms do eventually go away, so be patient and try not to rush back for more pills.

4. Don't expect antidepressant drugs to sort out your emotional problems. That's your job.

5. Don't think you can swallow pills and not adjust your lifestyle. That won't work either.

6. "Mix 'n' match" is for sweaters and skirts, not drugs. If you are being changed from one drug to another, ask your doctor if there should be a delay to get the first drug out of your system before you start the second. With some drugs this is not a problem, but with others (particularly MAOIs) it is. There should also be a gap of at least two weeks before you resume eating banned foods if you have been taking MAOIs.

## Light Treatment for Depression

Full-spectrum light treatment helps some people with depression, particularly in the dark winter months or in northern climes. Formerly, sufferers had to visit a hospital daily for this treatment, but now a portable light panel is available for use in the home. (Full-spectrum lighting is also discussed on page 50.) Daily exposure to this not only cures "winter blues" (SAD), but is also beneficial to general health, particularly the immune system.

## Herbs for Depression

### St. John's Wort (Hypericum perforatum)

This popular herbal supplement is taken by millions of people around the world as a "natural" way to beat the blues. St. John's Wort may act by inhibiting monoamine oxidase (MAO), the enzyme that breaks down serotonin and other chemicals in the brain. Or it may assist the action of serotonin itself. Clinical research studies in Europe suggest that St. John's Wort may be as effective as commonly prescribed drugs in treating mild to moderate depression—and have fewer side effects (although increased sensitivity to sun is one).

Look for a standardized extract that contains 0.3 percent hypericum. For the most benefit, take 300 mg two or three times a day, with meals. It should not be taken at bedtime, as it may have a slight stimulant effect. Some people drink one or two cups a day as a tea, and food manufacturers have begun adding small amounts of the herb to breakfast cereals, fruit drinks, canned soups, and other products. However, the Food and Drug Administration (FDA) has not given its approval for St. John's Wort to be used as a food additive.

The focus of the first federally funded, large-scale trial of an herbal supplement in the United States, a three-year study of St. John's Wort by the National Institute of Mental Health is about to end, with findings due in 2001.

## Valerian and Melatonin

Other herbs widely taken to alleviate depression are valerian (tea and extracts) and melatonin. Valerian is reputed to be a mild sedative. Melatonin is also used as a sleep aid for insomnia and taken to prevent jet lag. (See pages 28–29 for more information.)

As more truly scientific research is done, the benefits of herbs for depression will be better defined.

# CHAPTER TWELVE

# Physical Reasons for Anxiety and Depression

## Physical Causes of Nervous Feelings

These include: hormonal changes (puberty, premenstrual syndrome [PMS], childbirth, hysterectomy, menopause), certain glandular disorders (such as thyroid problems), anemia, infections, and chronic physical pain.

Some of these conditions may pose a "Which came first? the chicken or the egg?" puzzle—was it tired nerves causing bodily dysfunction, which in turn caused anxiety and depression, or the other way around?

### Body-Mind Interaction

It is agreed that the body affects the mind and the mind affects the body; but if someone is anxious or depressed, there is often a tendency to concentrate on looking for psychological causes and, as a result, physical causes can be overlooked. Even if the condition has been caused by stress, there are many instances where psychological help alone does not work, and unless the physical symptoms are also treated, the patient does not make progress.

## Allergies: Conditions Often Mistaken for "Nerves"

The word "allergy" has been around since the beginning of the century. It describes an altered reaction in the body tissue to a substance that is not normally poisonous. This is an allergic reaction.

The contact can be from eating, drinking, touching, or inhaling.

No one is surprised by familiar allergic reactions like hay fever or asthma, or even a severe reaction to some foods such as peanuts, chocolate, or milk products. What is more difficult to accept is that *many* people have chronic food or chemical allergies that produce multitudinous symptoms, including anxiety and depression. It is important that these be recognized as symptoms coming from one's altered brain chemistry (caused by allergens) and *not* from neurosis. All the psychological tricks in the book will not work if the cause of the change in mood is due to an allergy to wheat (or to anything else).

## Yeast Infections (Thrush—Chronic Candidiasis)

It has been acknowledged for close to twenty years that many drugs (including antibiotics, steroids, birth control pills, and more recently tranquilizers and sleeping pills) weaken the immune system and allow organisms normally present in the body to multiply rapidly. The fungus *Candida albicans* is one of them. It crowds out the good bacteria in the bowel and plays havoc with the digestive system. It produces numerous chemicals, including female hormones (in both males *and* females). This is probably one of the reasons for the mood swings and severe premenstrual tension experienced by so many women who have this problem.

Because chronic candidiasis (infection or disease caused by that fungus) produces so many symptoms, including anxiety and depression, it is often diagnosed as a psychosomatic (mind affecting the body) illness. People who have been incorrectly diagnosed have spent years going back and forth to psychiatric outpatient departments. The treatment they receive—more and more pills—makes matters worse, and many people have turned to alternative medicine for help. The body will often tell us what is wrong if we choose to "listen" to it. So many *candida* sufferers have said, "I *knew* something in my body was affecting my head."

Treatment is effective, although it can take several months and consists of antifungal agents (not always drugs), diet changes, and food supplements, including vitamins and minerals. Live yogurt cleans up the digestive tract and discourages the growth of the *candida*.

Although the *candida* problem is growing to enormous proportions, in general the medical world has been slow in recognizing what is happening. They tend to think that thrush *(candida)* only flourishes in the vagina or in babies' mouths.

## ENDLESS INVESTIGATIONS

Patients with *candida* (and/or allergies) often have full gastrointestinal workups (tubes poked into every possible place), and the results are invariably negative. The diagnosis is usually "irritable bowel syndrome"; this may simply mean: "I cannot find a cause for your symptoms." The high-fiber diet usually recommended always makes the symptoms worse. This is not surprising, since it would include foods that "feed" the yeast. There are several helpful books available that describe the anti*candida* diet fully. (See Further Reading and Reference, page 125.)

## CANDIDA SYMPTOMS COMMONLY REPORTED

*Abdominal*  Discomfort, bloating, gas, wakefulness, constipation/diarrhea, frequent cystitis that does not respond to antibiotics, vaginal discharge, infection in the penis with soreness and discharge, mouth infections, ear infections (often a watery discharge that makes the skin around the ear sore), depression, anxiety.

Other problems are nail bed infections, athlete's foot, scalp problems, sores in the nose, cracks at the side of the mouth, and coated sore tongue and inside of cheeks. The soft palate and throat can also be affected. In fact, some people say they feel inflamed from the mouth to the anus (which also becomes sore and itches).

*A sluggish colon*   Diets high in refined carbohydrates (such as white bread, sugar, and cakes or pastries), lack of exercise, and stress all contribute to the condition known as "toxic colon." This is a wonderful breeding ground for fungus *(candida)*. The bowel produces more mucus to rid itself of irritant foods, and the result is that this mucus binds with the refined carbohydrate to make a sticky layer that coats the lumen of the bowel. This layer of old feces can weigh up to eight pounds; it not only causes discomfort, but also blocks the absorption of essential minerals and vitamins and prevents the production of enzymes— those chemicals that are vital for the digestion of food.

*Urinary*   The *candida* fungus could be the cause of the endless cystitis seen in some "nervous" people. Cultures of their urine fail to produce organisms, while symptoms do not respond to antibiotics. Sugary and yeasty foods, as well as alcohol (wine, beer, and hard liquor), make the symptoms worse. Always see your doctor if you have persistent abdominal or urinary symptoms. If she can find nothing wrong (there is no reliable test for *candida*, and she is probably unlikely to think of investigating for this anyway), you might want to seek a doctor specializing in clinical nutrition. Unfortunately, this is rarely available under HMOs or traditional health insurance plans, so if money is a problem you can use self-help methods. The health of many people has dramatically improved after following the instructions in the *candida* books (see Further Reading and Reference, page 125).

*Fungal skin problems*   Such problems are sometimes mistaken for nervous rashes. These can appear as dry, scaly red patches appearing anywhere on the body, but more usually over the cheekbones, at the sides of the nose, by the ears, and on the hands.

*Food and chemical sensitivities*   Because the immune system is weakened, food and chemical allergies and *candida* often go together. Common complaints are: palpitations, flushes, headaches, lightheadedness, abdominal bloating, or breathlessness after eating certain foods or being near gasoline fumes, gas fires, and so on. There are a number of useful books on this subject to help you discover which foods are causing your problems by using elimination diets; they also suggest how to rid your home of unnecessary chemicals. If your symptoms are severe, it would be wise to seek professional help.

## Chronic Fatigue Syndrome (Myalgic Encephalomyelitis)

This is not a new disease. Symptoms of this chronic illness, which produces bouts of extreme tiredness in the muscles and brain, have been described for more than a century. It can start with an illness like glandular fever or flu; sometimes it is so severe that people have to give up work for a time. For decades, sufferers from this condition have been classed as malingerers or hypochondriacs. Myalgic encephalomyelitis (ME) was first recorded 50 years ago, but only in recent years has there been a sharing of information among sufferers and doctors. For a time it was thought to be linked to the Epstein-Barr virus, but that theory has now been discounted. ME is often mistaken for nervous illness because the symptoms include anxiety, depression, and lethargy; it is also sometimes called the "yuppie disease" or "malingerer's disease." (CFS is diagnosed two to four times as often in women as in men.) The immune system is also affected, and multiple allergies and *candida* can be present.

Research is presently being carried out, but as yet there is no answer to be found in conventional medicine. Complementary medicine has helped many people recover completely. The important aspects of treatment are rest, a healthy diet, fresh air, daylight, keeping the bowel as clean as possible by preventing constipation, and restoring a normal balance to the gut bacteria. Any therapy that promotes relaxation and natural healing is also recommended. Doctors often prescribe antidepressants, but they rarely help this condition; they merely add more poisons to a body already struggling hard to excrete the poisons caused by the virus. Some people improve with a course of the tricyclic antidepressants. The reason for this is unknown. (See Further Reading and Reference, page 125.)

## Chronic Pain as a Cause of Nervous Exhaustion

It is not only the discomfort of pain that affects the nerves, but also the continual tension in the muscles. The person with even mild chronic pain never completely relaxes. Remember the firefighter: when he tenses his muscles and increases his breathing rate, his adrenaline levels go up. If this is repeated over and over again—whatever the cause— anxiety, irritability, and other nervous symptoms can result. People in pain often overbreathe in an attempt to control the pain. How this affects anxiety levels is discussed in Chapter Sixteen.

# Nutritional Deficiencies as a Cause of Anxiety and Depression

When the nerves are under stress, the body has an enormously increased need for particular vitamins and minerals. Poor appetite and faulty absorption often result in severe depletion of these vital substances. Even if you are a comfort eater and quite weighty, you can still be lacking in minerals and vitamins.

## Common Signs of Vitamin Deficiencies

1. A tongue that is: swollen/sore/smooth/shiny red, sore and bright-red at the tip, swollen taste buds, patches like a map, deeply fissured, swollen veins under the tongue.

2. Bleeding gums, mouth ulcers, gum boils, cracks at the corners of the mouth, peeling lips, recurrent cold sores (herpes).

3. Slow healing of wounds, altered taste sensation, bruising easily, falling hair.

4. Cramps and tired muscles.

These symptoms usually respond quickly to the correct supplements. Consult your doctor to see if he can guide you, or read one of the many books on the subject, such as *Nutritional Medicine* (see Further Reading and Reference, page 125).

It is important to follow guidelines because you could create more problems if you don't. For example: long-term continuous use of vitamin $B_6$ can cause neurological problems; large doses of vitamin D are toxic; and vitamin B complex can be a strong stimulant—fine if you are depressed, but not if you are anxious and sleepless. Some vitamin B complexes (often ones containing yeast) can also cause cystitis, abdominal bloating, skin rashes, and itching around the anus. Supplementation with calcium and magnesium (plus chromium if you have blood-sugar problems) can be of great benefit to the nervous system.

*Depression and food*   An overacid body can encourage low mood. A diet high in refined carbohydrates and meat makes for high acid levels, while an eating plan that includes large amounts of vegetables, particularly raw, and complex carbohydrates makes the body more alkaline. (See *Raw Energy* by Leslie and Susannah Kenton [Century Arrow, 1984].)

Nervous symptoms often take a physical form. We have seen that certain bodily functions are particular targets for anxiety and depression. In some people the fear, anger, and sadness they experience comes out in physical symptoms. This is called somatizing. There is often an unhappy memory that causes symptoms to be "laid down" in a particular place. The event is often recalled when tension is released, say in a shoulder, during physical therapy such as massage. The astonished patient comes in with a sore shoulder, which he sees as entirely physical, and ends up crying about a sad or frightening incident that happened in the distant past. Take away the tension, and the emotional pain can be released.

Here are some examples of how releasing emotional pain can help alleviate physical pain.

One young man came for help with a pain in his right knee, although it was clear he was also a little depressed. The pain (and depression) had come and gone for years. He had not mentioned the depression to his doctor; in fact, he did not realize the feeling was depression. He had his knee examined several times, but the cause of the pain remained a mystery. During his therapy he remembered being slapped continually by his mother as he sat by her in the car. When he jumped around or argued with his brother (who was in the back seat), his left knee took the punishment. When he recalled this, he became very angry and said, "She is not going to slap me down this time." After he announced his engagement his mother became cold and distant. It was then that his symptoms returned. His emotional progress was slow, although his knee improved rapidly. At first he felt a lot of anxiety when he started to express his feelings—he felt he was hurting his mother. Who had been hurting him for years? She gave him a lot of love and approval, yes, but only if he lived his life in accordance with her wishes. He was a gentle person, and the thought of open, honest communication worried him. He was finally convinced that it could be done with love, and indeed had to be done, if he wanted to be well and live his own life.

One young woman had a cancer phobia: her mother had died from cancer of the bowel when she was 29. The woman was approaching this age, and was convinced that the same fate awaited her. For several years she had complained of abdominal pain, and was jumping on and off the scales about seven times a day to see if she had lost weight. The negative result of numerous tests still could not convince her that she had no organic disease. By sharing her feelings with others, she could eventually see that tension was causing her abdominal discomfort and she lost all her symptoms. She gained ten pounds and started playing tennis.

These are only illustrations of how emotional pain can be released. It is not always necessary to have a therapist or join a group. Loosening up your body with swimming, yoga, or other exercise can have the same effect (see Part Two).

# CHAPTER THIRTEEN

# Misdiagnosis

Being misdiagnosed can be very hurtful for patients. Negative remarks from a physician or health-care practitioner can eat away at patients' self-esteem and fill them with self-doubt. Have any of these unhelpful comments ever been directed at you?

- "Pull yourself together."

- "You are just anxious."

- "You're merely depressed."

- "You enjoy the attention of being ill."

- "The pain you feel is hysterical."

- "This is all in your head."

Incidentally, the next time anyone tells you to pull yourself together, smile and say, "I would really like to do that. Can you tell me how I can do it?" It is unlikely that they would have any valid answers for you. Of course there are those who malinger, but for those who don't —people with nervous troubles longing to be well—it seems very unjust to keep pointing the finger at them. They have a double burden to endure: their distressing symptoms, plus the degradation of being told: "You enjoy ill health." There seems to be little to enjoy in having so much sick leave that you lose your job, are never without discomfort, and become a constant source of anxiety to those around you.

Take the following example: Ruth, a 30-year-old computer programmer, had complained of abdominal pain on and off for four years. She felt the doctor was dismissing her because she had shown a history of nervous troubles in her early twenties.

The nagging pain dragged her down, as did the "Are *you* here again!" look she was given during her regular visits to the clinic. She tried every doctor in the practice. One prescribed antidepressants. These gave her headaches, she gained 13 pounds, and the premenstrual tension she had always suffered became unbearable. She continued to complain of abdominal pain and was eventually sent to a specialist. Investigative surgery revealed that she had a notoriously painful gynecological (womb) condition, corrected medically.

Years later, she cried bitterly during a counseling session, saying that not one person had said, "Sorry, you were right," or "That was bad luck."

## People Who Do Invent Their Symptoms

It cannot be denied that this does happen, and it is a source of irritation to those around; but surely, in many instances, the person who exaggerates or invents physical pain needs as much attention as the person with an obvious physical problem. He is like a child who says his leg hurts, when in reality he has a very sore throat—he cannot localize his pain. He knows he is hurting, but he is not sure where.

Invented pain is usually treated as a moral issue—someone trying to deceive. It may be deception, but not at a conscious level. If people are not hurting, then there is no pain, and they simply get on with their lives. Perhaps we have grown up with the idea that physical pain is the only allowable pain. So many people say they have no trouble canceling an engagement if they have a cold or sore throat, but feel anxiety and guilt if they have to change arrangements because they are too depressed to function. They often invent something physical and then worry about the lie, or feel degraded because they have had "flu" once again.

The boy who goes to his father showing him a bloodied knee is likely to have the wound washed, doctored up, and covered with a bandage. What would happen if the child went to his father and said he was afraid or sad: "*Afraid?* Big boys of seven aren't afraid," or "What have you got to be *sad* about? We're going camping next week after school's out." Emotional pain? All a little embarrassing, really. Is it any wonder the therapists' appointment books are full?

# PART TWO
## Self-help Therapy for Anxiety and Depression

# CHAPTER FOURTEEN

# Being Your Own Therapist

You may feel you do not need outside help and want to see how much progress you can make on your own. The results can often be dramatic when people start to love themselves, give up pretending, and really learn how to relax.

Two processes can happen spontaneously even when you are not having professional treatment: *catharsis* (the cleansing of the effects of pent-up emotions by bringing them to the surface of consciousness) and *abreaction* (the resolution of a neurosis by reviving forgotten or repressed ideas of the event that first caused it). It can be a little alarming if you don't know what is happening, but it should be welcomed. You will feel better as a result of it. The example of Paula, below, illustrates this trigger effect.

Paula's marriage was happy and she enjoyed her part-time work. She had suffered periods of depression all her life, although they were not disabling enough for her to seek help; she could still function. She went to a therapist for help when she was confused and depressed after her mother died.

She felt she was grieving normally for her, but was surprised by her mounting feelings of hate for her father. He had been dead for some years, and she thought she had forgotten about how miserable he had made her young life. She started to dream about him and would wake up feeling depressed. He filled her waking thoughts for days, and she could not even escape from him in sleep.

She was feeling particularly strung-out with premenstrual tension one day as she was coming home from work. The sound of piano-playing came through an open window. The memory it brought back made her feel sick with rage: she was nine years old, and being shaken violently by her father; he was angry because she was reluctant to practice the piano. Her timid mother always urged her to keep quiet and not upset her father.

After a few days of being restless and tearful, everything poured out. Her astonished husband came home to find her shouting abuse at her absent father for his cruelty, and to her absent mother for not protecting her. She was tearing up an old boxful of sheet music.

After the "confetti" had stopped flying, she dissolved into tears, and said she felt a great sense of release; she now no longer needed to keep quiet about her misery. She could get rid of it. Although she knew her actions seemed childish, she continued expressing them because of the great sense of satisfaction they brought. Discharging so much pent-up emotion left her drained, yet feeling that she was true to herself for the first time in her life.

## Cognitive Therapy—
## The "Change Your Thinking" Approach

This treatment helps to overcome restrictions in everyday life by breaking the vicious circle of negative thoughts. Fear-provoking thoughts are changed by repeatedly replacing them with positive encouragement. Cognitive therapy takes various forms, as follows.

### Self-Talk

This is just what the name implies. By repeating instructions to ourselves, either aloud or quietly, we can break negative thinking habits.

If you were learning to play a new piece on the clarinet and stumbled repeatedly at the same phrase, practicing over and over again would correct the fault. We can do the same with our thoughts. It often helps to write them down and to practice replacing negative thoughts with positive thoughts when you are relaxed, so that they become automatic when you are in troubling situations. For example, someone who is afraid of authority could practice intoning (mentally or out loud): "I don't need to be afraid of people in charge any longer. I am not a child now, I am safe, my confidence is growing. . . ."

Choose any of the statements below that you feel are appropriate for you, and add others that would be helpful. Write them down on index cards, in your day-planner, or on pieces of paper. (You might want to think twice, though, about posting them on the refrigerator or in your office cubicle.)

1. This crazy need to talk all the time means I am uptight and need to relax more.

2. I will be patient with myself. I will be in charge again.

3. Am I making this panic worse—am I hungry, angry, lonely, tired or breathing badly, or something? (Put this card in several places: on the fridge, on the bathroom mirror, on the television set. . . .)

4. Don't moan on and on—you know how stupid you feel afterward. (This card should go by the telephone.)

5. This is not my normal behavior. It will go. I have everything I need inside myself to get better. Every day in every way I am getting better and better. I am a wonderful person. I deserve good health.

Have you identified which fear is dragging you down? Some common ones are: death, authority, injury, illness, growing old, being alone, failure, success, responsibility, personal relationships, sexuality.

## Negative Thoughts

Do some of your wayward thoughts also come from unrealistic expectations of how you or other people "should" behave? Have they crept up on you, and are they now so strong that they are affecting your life?

*What are your expectations of others?* How often are your demands un-reasonable: "I must be loved all the time"/"If they don't do as I say, then they don't love me"/"If he doesn't notice when I'm tired, or when my shoes are worn out, then he can't love me"/"If she doesn't agree with everything I say, then she is against me"/"I need total commit-ment in a relationship (does this mean total control?)."

*What are your expectations of yourself?* "If I lose my temper no one will love me"/"If I don't look my best he will not love me"/"If I don't do everything she wants, she will leave me"/"If I don't get good grades she will not love me"/"If I don't go home for Christmas she will think I don't love her"/"I must not be seen to be wrong"/"I must not show weakness."

*Can you have too much reassurance and support?* Ill people often need to be dependent for a time, but if this carries on too long it can stop their recovering—a similar effect to prolonged drug therapy. The strain of having to uphold a nervous person for long periods can also have a serious effect on the health of the relatives or significant others.

## People Dependency

People who are trapped by fearful or negative thoughts often seek con-stant reassurance. This affords only temporary relief, and the sufferer wants more and more. This could be termed reassurance neurosis or people dependency. This happens not only in the therapeutic situa-tion, but also in personal relationships. Some people become so de-pendent on their partner, they cannot bear them to leave their side for a minute. This often puts a great strain on the marriage or relation-ship. The sufferer thinks only of how fearful they are and even insists that the partner stays awake if they cannot sleep. Sometimes the suf-ferer refuses to be in the house alone and the partner has to arrange for a "baby sitter."

If you feel your partner is being hard on you, it is much better to say so even if you risk their tears or anger. It is neither realistic nor helpful to take it all and say nothing, no matter how sympathetic you feel.

It is also very important not to let the sufferer talk endlessly about how they feel. Insist that they talk about symptoms only at certain times, say for ten minutes after dinner. They will be very angry at first and say you are unfeeling. Point out to them that they need to reach out to normality—it won't just land in their lap.

*Treatment for people dependency*    The cognitive therapist encourages people to avoid seeking external sources of reassurance, teaching them the importance of reassuring themselves. Of course, it is unrealistic to expect sufferers to do this if you don't teach them to understand their nerves and how to relax.

Nothing can be more demoralizing than to need someone with you, or to need to be on the phone constantly, in order to get through the day. Use self-talk to cure this habit.

# CHAPTER FIFTEEN

# Working with Your Body—Relaxation

## Work with the Body to Help Your Nerves

How tight muscles cause anxiety was discussed earlier (Chapter Three). You may think: "I will just relax them and the anxiety levels will come down." Unfortunately, it is not as easy as that. The muscles are in the habit of tightening up, and you may not be aware of this until you realize you are walking around with your shoulders around your ears or your head pushed forward like a turtle. And here's the bad news: you are going to have to be constantly vigilant until your muscles are retrained. It is an interesting comment (from Dr. Joe McDonald) that panic attacks are easily induced in normal people by injecting lactate, a common by-product of overstressed muscle tissue.

## Become Aware of How You Are Using Your Body

### The Head

Your head is heavier than you might imagine—about 20 pounds. If it is unbalanced it can affect the whole body. When you are anxious or depressed, the muscles that run down the side of the neck (the ster-nomastoids) tend to become contracted or shortened, affecting your breathing, as well as the head, neck, shoulders, and all the way down the spine, through the pelvis, even causing tension in the legs.

*How to balance the head:* Sit on a chair with the spine straight, but not taut; look a few feet in front of you at the floor (if your eyes are down you cannot shorten the muscles at the side of the neck); keep your shoulders down; now raise your eyes enough to comfortably look around the room—this is the balanced position for your head. The chin is pointing downward, not poking out in front. Whoever taught us to keep our back straight, head up, shoulders back and chin up, did us a great disservice. It is an unnatural position for the head and spine.

## The Alexander Technique

This technique is one of the most successful methods of learning cor-rect posture and how to move without tension.

It trains the body to move in a way that reduces stress and results in better posture. It can be helpful in many illnesses or after injury. The method is very gentle and concentrates on guiding the pupil's move-ments until he becomes aware of his bad habits. If you have a teacher near you, it would be money well spent to take a few classes.

For more information see Further Reading and Reference, page 125.

## Quick Tension Relief

This can be done anywhere—on a bus, in a friend's house, at your desk in the office. No one needs to know what you are doing.

Sit with your head balanced as described above: drop your shoulders; imagine they are a coathanger and that your body is a wet garment hanging from it. Check your head again, and then shake your arms and place them palms upward in your lap. Squeeze your thighs to-gether, and then let them fall back into position. Cross your ankles loosely and let the knees fall apart, or just place the feet flat on the floor.

## Relaxation Lying Down—Five or Ten Minutes

This is best done on the floor, but can be done on the bed. Lying down increases the blood supply to the head (you will know this if you have ever had a toothache), takes the force of gravity off the spine, and gives the heart a rest. It takes a lot of energy to stay upright. Lying down also allows all your bones to fall into a natural position. We have seen that the relaxation response is more efficient after exercise. Here is a very quick exercise to do before lying down.

## The Wet-Dog Exercise

Simply open your mouth and shake all over like a dog throwing water from his coat. Hold the wall or a chair and shake each leg. This is also a good exercise for people who are worried about shaking (through nerves) in public. It takes much *more* energy to hold back the shaking than to have a really good shake. If you are out in public and are embarrassed by shaking, go into a restroom and make yourself shake all over. After that, you may not be able to shake even if you wanted to!

Make sure the room is not too cold or stuffy and have a blanket or coat nearby. Some people become very cold as they relax; others feel tingly and warm. A feeling of heaviness is usual, although some people say they feel light-bodied and light-headed. Ignore all these feelings. If you are very tense, this routine should be as important in your day as brushing your teeth (do the wet-dog shake twice daily: on waking, and before the evening meal).

## The Tighten-and-Let-Go Method

It is better to avoid the tighten-and-let-go method of relaxation, which asks you to tighten and relax each group of muscles in turn. If you are very tense, and particularly if you are withdrawing from drugs or alcohol, you can increase your discomfort by following this routine, as the muscles can go into spasm. It can be very uncomfortable if the wide muscle in the back (latissimus dorsi) contracts. You feel your back is arched and you cannot lie flat.

## Longer Relaxation Session

Use the following routine:

1. Lie on the floor, raise your head 3 or 4 inches with something firm underneath like paperback books, bend your knees and have your feet flat on the floor (this is important if you have back trouble); if you have a good back and want to stretch out, do so after a couple of minutes.

2. Take one deep breath through the nose. Imagine that your whole body is being filled with air, and then slacken the jaw and let the air slowly out through the mouth. Feel that you are sinking through the floor.

3. Mentally stroke each part of your body in turn and say to yourself three times each:

   —My right arm is heavy.

   —My left arm is heavy.

   —My right leg is heavy.

   —My left leg is heavy.

   —My whole body is heavy and comfortable.

4. Now go over the body again, mentally stroking, and this time saying:

   —My right arm is warm.

   —My left arm is warm, and so on.

5. Finish with:

   —My whole body is warm.

6. Now imagine a pure white light filling you with energy. Stretch, and wriggle your fingers and toes. Turn onto your side, and then sit up. Wait for a moment before slowly standing up.

This is a simple routine, but don't be surprised if your body does not respond too well at first. It may take some practice. You cannot force yourself into a relaxed state, for trying to do so will make you tighten up even more. Just keep going through the exercise each day and it will come. You may notice that some muscles ache a little when you get up from the floor—they have had the benefit of an increased blood supply. This is a good sign! It means that your body has let go and the joints have been allowed to go into a different position. When you were a child did you ever tie a string or rubber band around the end of your finger? The end goes numb. When you take the band off, the blood rushes back and the finger can ache for a few seconds. This is what has happened in your muscles.

## Using Your Body Without Tension—Be Aware

### What Am I Doing with My Head and Neck?

Am I holding my head on one side?

Am I in the turtle position?

Am I pulling it back and sticking my chin up?

Do I strain my neck by turning it repeatedly to one side?

Do I have to turn it to watch TV, to look out the window?

Do I chew only on one side? (Are there dental problems to correct?)

### What Am I Doing with My Shoulders?

Are my shoulders around my ears?

Is one shoulder higher than the other?

Am I curving one or both shoulders toward the front of my body?

Am I fiercely gripping: my pen, the steering wheel, the golf club, my tools, my computer mouse, my knitting needles…?

Am I pulling my shoulders up or holding my head on one side when I talk, wash dishes, travel…?

## What Else Am I Doing?

Are my arms tightly folded over my chest? Do I cross my legs at the knee, then tuck the foot of the crossed leg behind the other ankle, almost as if in a knot? (We do this to protect ourselves from the outside world and to keep our hurts and fears to ourselves.)

Are my fists clenched tightly all the time? Am I gripping my fork as if it were a pistol?

Am I pulling my thumb into an unnatural position?

Do I press my arms fiercely to my sides?

Am I afraid to really use my breathing muscles?

Am I tightening my stomach? (This is the cause of a great many problems.)

When a doctor is examining a patient with an inflamed appendix, the sufferer contracts his muscles over the sore place to protect it from the pressure of the doctor's fingers. This is called "guarding." We do the same with our emotional pain.

## Gut Feelings

The solar plexus is a collection of nerves just below the diaphragm near the stomach and liver. This area is often called the seat of the emotions. Think of some of the expressions we use: gut feelings, I can feel it in my gut, he dealt me a body blow, hitting below the belt, she got me in the solar plexus. Tension in the abdomen can cause ulcers, constipation, and menstrual problems, among many others.

If you want a healthy inside, you will have to let these muscles relax. It is necessary to work on all the muscles, but the muscles of the abdomen are particularly important because they also affect the breathing. We shall see in Chapter 16 how vital it is to breathe correctly.

*Exercise for the solar plexus*   When you are lying on the floor or bed:

> Imagine that your stomach is the sea and on it is a boat with a blue sail. Lift the boat up on a large wave, breathing in through your nose, slowly but not deeply. Let the boat fall gently as you breathe out. Just do this once, and don't worry if your heart thumps a little.

> Now with the lightest touch possible, rub your stomach 60 times in a clockwise direction. This is a helpful exercise for people with a lot of gas.

## What Am I Doing with My Lower Body?

- Am I tensing my thighs because I have a fear of not making it to the bathroom in time?

- Am I tightening up the muscles in the pelvic floor because I don't want to admit to sexual feelings?

- Am I tightening up my legs when I walk because I wear the wrong shoes—or because I really don't want to go out?

## Using the Body Symmetrically

When you have discovered where you are holding your tension, the next step is to work out how much the way you are moving is aggravating the problem (or indeed causing it). Make sure you use both sides of the body. For instance, don't always carry shopping bags or your backpack or briefcase on the same side, and don't reach up to cupboards or pick up the newspaper off the porch with the same arm.

It's worth taking care of your muscles, because nervous people cannot even relax during sleep and often complain of aching and stiffness all over. They wake even more tired than when they went to bed.

# Massage

If muscles are contracted with tension, not only are they denied essential nutrients, but also the waste products from metabolism (how the body uses food) are not flushed out and carried away. This builds up in the form of crystals rather like soap building up in laundry that is not adequately rinsed. This is why you can feel pain when someone is massaging your shoulders. When the muscle is pressed onto the bone the crystals (toxins) can be felt. If the muscles are not moved, the aching and stiffness will persist. Exercise will increase circulation and help to disperse the crystals, but you will get quicker results if you use massage as well. This does not have to be done by a professional. Anyone can do simple massage, and if you watch the following points you cannot do any harm:

- Do not massage over broken skin or varicose veins.

- Do not press deeply into an inflamed muscle; use a very light touch.

- Do not massage the front of the neck, breasts, or stomach.

Be aware that massaging the front of the neck can cause fainting, from pressure on the main blood vessels; massage of breasts can cause arousal; massage of the abdomen may cause an urgent need to use the bathroom. To massage these areas you would need professional training.

As long as you have followed these rules, try to turn your mind off, relax, and let your hands do the work. People who have been tense for a long time are very surprised that they can feel so much more comfortable around the neck and shoulders after even a short massage.

There are a few people who are anxious about relaxing their shoulders, fearing they will "go to pieces" or fall over without the support of their "armor."

## Working On the Neck and Shoulders

You do not need to know the person you are working with, and in fact it is often better if you don't.

If you massage regularly either for a friend or in a group, your fingers will soon become sensitive to the feeling of the muscles before and after a session.

*Instructions for the sufferer:* Some people (usually those who have cared for others all their lives) find it very difficult to allow their partner to help. Just be—without worrying. Imagine you are a rag doll. Your helper is not in the least interested in whether your outfit came from Bloomingdale's or how long it is since you washed your hair. She is interested in your discomfort and how she can help.

*Instructions for the helper:* Be as relaxed as you can; let your breath out as you drop your shoulders; feel the desire to help your partner. Sit your partner on an upright chair. Stand behind her; make sure that her back is straight but slack (use cushions if necessary to make her comfortable), press her shoulders down, and check the position of her head.

1. Support her forehead with one hand and with the other move the muscles of the scalp just as if you were washing her hair.

2. Continue to support the forehead; massage quite firmly at the base of the skull using the thumb and fingers to make small circular movements.

3. Now move onto the back of the neck, using the thumb and index finger on either side of the neck bones, again using a circular movement.

4. Place your hands over the shoulders and use the thumb or heel of the hand to knead the muscles in a circular motion; ask if there are any places needing extra attention.

5. Put one arm across the top of your partner's chest and encourage her to relax forward onto it. With the other hand, continue massaging down the side of (but not on) the bones of the spine. Work in a similar fashion around the shoulder blade. Use the other arm and repeat for the other side of spine.

6. Stand in front of your partner, pick up the wrist and shake the hand, letting it flop (unless there is pain in

the joint), and ask her to imagine being a wet sweater hanging outdoors on the clothesline. You will feel the arm become heavier when she thinks "heavy." Give the arm a little shake, and then do the same for the other hand and arm.

7. Stand behind your partner, support her head against your chest, and stroke the brow (eyes closed) with both first fingers from the center outward.

8. Finish off by stroking lightly and rapidly from the head down the back and then down the arms and hands.

Sometimes people are quite sleepy after a head and neck massage. Your partner might need a short rest before helping you.

It is a great help if a very tense person can have a massage daily. The therapeutic value of massage is becoming more recognized in this country. Aromatherapy—massaging with the essential oil of plants—has also been proved to have a beneficial effect on the nervous system (see Further Reading and Reference, page 125).

## Getting the Circulation Going

When the firefighter is fighting the fire, his adrenaline levels are very high, but because he is so active he is burning off the excess. He can relax when his work is finished. Some people are so anxious, they are afraid to move—thinking they must reserve their energy just to get through the day; others say, "I get enough exercise; I'm so wound up I rush around like a chicken with its head cut off." Rushing around in a constant state of tension is almost as bad as not having any exercise; the adrenaline levels are not worked off by the effort, because they are continually being "refilled" by tension (just as a waterfall refills a pool).

### If You Are Depressed, Get Moving. Exercise!

If you are very depressed, you might have so little energy that it is difficult to drag yourself from the bed to the chair; recovery will be much quicker if you start moving. It will be a terrible effort at first, but it will not harm you.

## *Exercises Sitting on a Chair*

1. Balance your head (see page 86), take one deep breath, lifting your shoulders as you do so; open your mouth as you let the breath out and drop your shoulders. Feel like a pricked balloon.

2. Breathe normally, lift the shoulders toward the ears and let them drop eight times.

3. Keeping the arm limp, circle each shoulder in a clockwise direction eight times, and then try doing them together.

4. Stretch both arms to the ceiling without straining, and let them fall loosely toward the floor.

5. Stretch out the fingers, and then draw eight circles each way with the forefingers.

6. To exercise the legs, draw the same circles with each big toe in turn.

7. If you are not too tired, stand up and do any loose swinging movement you can think of.

8. Finish with the wet-dog shake.

Don't let it stop there: see how many gentle stretching exercises you can incorporate into your daily routine. For example, walk upstairs on your toes to stretch the backs of your legs, reach up to shelves with both hands, hold the stretch and then relax. Do loose swinging movements, running on the spot, or the wet-dog shake, when you are waiting for the pasta to boil or while talking on the phone. Before getting into the bath tub, hold the side of the tub and bend your knees a few times; rotate your ankles or massage your hands as you watch television.

Building these movements into your daily routine is useful if you do not feel up to swimming, walking, yoga, or other activities. Remember what happens to your circulation if you don't move.

# Meditation and Yoga

## *Meditation*

Meditation can be a profound tool for dissolving the root causes of anxiety and depression. It helps develop clarity, stability, calmness, tolerance, and a positive outlook on life. While the basics of meditation can be introduced in a single sentence and safely explored on your own, it often helps to have a teacher or an experienced friend to consult when questions or difficulties arise. Many people also find that meditating with a group provides a sense of support and relief from some of the distractions that inevitably arise.

There are many forms of meditation—some make use of a repeated word or phrase, some employ an object for the eyes to rest on, some advocate visualizing colors or light. Any of these methods can be effective, and some may suit your temperament better than others, but for many purposes, the following basic breathing meditation is the best place to start. Lest you think its directness and simplicity render it inferior, consider that the Buddha—an ancient scientist of human psychology—relied on this method himself and described it as sufficient to untangle the most complex suffering.

Find a quiet place where you won't be disturbed for half an hour. Sit comfortably, with your back straight but not rigid (a chair is fine, but keep your back straight), and pay attention to your breathing. Notice the air as it enters your nose, follow it as it goes down into your chest and back out your nostrils. That's it, basically. Breathe through your nose; pay attention to the air going in and out. It's better not to force your breath but you can try to slow it and deepen it if that helps you follow it. You can let your eyes be closed or half-open and unfocused (the breath is what you're focusing on).

You'll notice thoughts have arrived without any invitation. Some of them are interesting and you follow them without intending to. Don't worry about it—it's just the nature of mind to contrive distractions. When you notice you've been distracted by thoughts, simply let them depart and return your attention to your breath. Or you may feel sleepy (some people use meditation to help them sleep, though you can be sure there are more profound reasons to meditate than this). Again, notice that you've nodded off and return your awareness to your breathing, in and out.

Sometimes a question helps bring your attention back to the breath: Is this breath shallow? Is this breath deep? It would be easy to spend your whole time asking questions, so rather than be distracted by endless questions, choose one (be arbitrary: you'll have a chance to ask another question tomorrow) and ask it if you need a reminder to pay attention to your breathing.

You may feel some tightness or discomfort in various parts of your body. It's okay to shift your position slightly to relieve tension (you may find your body doing this on its own—when it does, try to be aware of it), but eventually you'll be able to simply note that there's a bit of discomfort (and where it is) and return your attention to the breath moving in and out of your body. As for those thoughts: they will come and go—that's what thoughts do. They may be saying all sorts of nasty, critical things, reminding you of tasks you *really* need to attend to, confusing you, making you worry that you're not doing it right. Don't worry: you're doing it right. Remind the thoughts that this is your time to be alone with your breathing. They'll come back again and again, but as you keep tuning in to that breath beneath the clamor you'll notice, sooner or later, that there's more space between thoughts, the breathing feels calmer, the attention easier to focus.

It's crucial to practice meditation consistently and frequently in order to realize its full benefits. While most teachers recommend at least an hour a day (which could be divided between morning and evening), even a consistent, daily session of 15 or 20 minutes at a time can help you develop calmness, understanding, and the sense that good things are possible.

## Yoga

As with meditation, yoga is most effective when practiced regularly —the cumulative effects of practicing a brief sequence every day easily surpass those of a gung-ho once-in-a-while, half-day workout. The point is consistency, which gives you a chance to adjust to subtle changes in your body and mind and integrate them into your daily life.

In the West, what most people know of as yoga is *hatha* yoga—the yoga of physical postures and breathing exercises. While an important branch of yoga, this is merely one of many ways of approaching what all yoga ultimately seeks to do, which is to unify body and mind, human and divine spirit, earth and heaven (the word yoga means "union" and is closely related to the English words "yoke" and "join"). It isn't necessary—or possible—to explore every variety of yoga, but if you're curious or inspired it's worth looking into further (any good hatha yoga teacher should be able to suggest resources). Since hatha yoga is the most widely represented in the West, it's a great place to start, and there's no substitute for a good instructor, of which there are many in all parts of the world. Once you get started with the basic postures and breathing, it's possible to practice on your own, and the benefits manifest quickly. Longtime yoga practitioners have not only greater flexibility, strength, and balance, but youthful vitality and vigor beyond what we normally expect from our human form—not to mention peace of mind.

The following exercise—Salute to the Sun—combines six yoga postures in a sequence of movements, and is traditionally done first thing in the morning to greet the day.

1. Stand with your feet together, knees straight, back stretched up but not tense. Place the palms of your hands together in front of your chest and breathe in slowly and deeply. Breathe out as you move into the second position.

2. Bend forward from the hips until your hands are on the ground a short distance in front of you. Move your hands forward until your legs are straight. Tuck in your chin toward your chest and pull your stomach in. Then breathe in as you move into the third position.

3. Keeping your hands and arms in the same place, stretch one foot as far as you can behind you. At the

same time, bend your other knee and bringing it forward between your arms, lifting up your head and slightly arching your back. Breathe out as you move to the fourth position.

4. Take your other foot back level with the first and straighten both legs. Try to press your heels toward the ground. Drop your head down so that your chin is tucked into your chest. Keep your arms straight and try to flatten and extend your spine. Take another breath in and breathe out as you go into the fifth position.

5. Keeping your hands and feet where they are, bend your arms and lower your body to the ground, touching the ground with your toes, knees, chest, and forehead. Pull your stomach in as you breathe out.

6. As you breathe in, lift up your head and bend backward, straightening your arms and legs so that the weight of your whole body is on your hands and toes.

7. As you breathe out, lift your bottom into the air, drop your head, tuck your chin in toward your chest, and straighten your legs. (This is the same as position four.)

8. As you breathe in, bring one leg forward so that the foot rests as closely as possible between your hands. Look up and bend back as in position three. Breathe out fully as you move into position nine.

9. Bring the other foot forward next to the first. Straighten your legs and tuck your chin in. (This is a repeat of position two.)

10. Breathe in as you lift your hands off the ground and stand up with a straight back. Join the palms in front of your chest.

You can repeat the sequence as many times as you like, though it is best to start gradually. (This variation of Salute to the Sun is taken from *Yoga* by Sophy Hoare.)

# Improving Circulation by Stimulating the Skin

In depression, boosting the circulation not only helps to normalize brain chemistry, but also helps the body to excrete toxins.

## Skin Brushing

If you brush yourself all over with a dry skin-brush (or bath brush) for about ten minutes before your bath or shower, you will greatly stimulate your circulation, help the release of toxins, and improve the texture of your skin. Avoid tender or broken skin, moles, and pimples. After a few days you will notice how the normally roughened areas such as knees, feet, and elbows become smoother and softer. You can use a softer small brush for the face, but avoid the tender area around the eyes.

# Water Therapies

Water has been known for thousands of years to be a great healer. Without even considering it as a therapy, how often do we gravitate to a hot bath to relax tense muscles or to a cool shower to stimulate us if we are feeling listless?

## Foot Baths

The skin of the feet has a tremendous number of nerve endings, therefore it is not surprising that reflexology is so effective. A daily self-foot massage for about ten minutes can also be helpful; or use an electric foot-massager. Massage calms the nervous system and aids both relaxation and the elimination of toxins. When you first try this, you will notice tender areas on the feet. As you continue to massage, the tenderness decreases. You may feel hardness or grittiness in these areas, which you can disperse with continued massage.

You could also try stamping in cold water in the bath (for safety, use a rubber bath mat) for three to five minutes. Better still, walk at the edge of the ocean (cold water, plus massage from sand and pebbles). This massages the soles of the feet and stimulates the hypothalamus gland, which increases the metabolic rate and produces a feeling of well-being.

## Detoxification by Heat

The profuse sweating of a fever is nature's way of detoxifying the body. You can do this artificially in Turkish baths and saunas, or at home in baths of salt, Epsom salts (magnesium), or seaweed. These are all available in large packs from most pharmacists or health food stores. A rough guide is to use about 2 pounds of salt, 3 cups full of Epsom salts, or 1 cupful of seaweed in a warm bath. The latter must be mixed to a paste in cold water and gradually added. Wrap up in a warm towel (if you have a radiator, towel warmer, or space heater in the bathroom), and rest for half an hour after your bath. Saunas and whirlpool baths or jacuzzis are also helpful for relaxation, though you should not stay in extremely hot water for very long.

# CHAPTER SIXTEEN

# Hyperventilation

To hyperventilate or overbreathe is to breathe in a rapid, shallow way using the upper chest instead of the abdomen. Breathing this way produces more oxygen than the body needs, and the result is a fall in carbon dioxide levels in the blood. This causes a multitude of symptoms that can mimic most known diseases. It can complicate the picture where there is organic disease, and it can also be the cause of endless fruitless investigations: neurological workups, heart tests, barium enemas, and on and on.

## How Hyperventilating Affects the Body

Since the normal functioning of every system in the body depends on the correct amount of oxygen and carbon dioxide circulating in the blood, it is easy to see why this "unbalanced blood" creates such havoc. Although formerly it was thought that anxiety caused hyperventilation, it is now known that it can be the other way round. L. C. Lum, consultant chest physician, Papworth Hospital in Cambridge,

# Symptoms of Hyperventilation

- General exhaustion

- Aching muscles

- Panic attacks

- Feelings of unreality

- Depersonalization
  (a feeling of not being
  you; your image looks
  strange in the mirror;
  you feel very detached
  from yourself)

- Dizziness

- Faintness

- Irritability

- Depression

- Free-floating anxiety

- Poor memory

- Lack of concentration

- Shortness of breath;
  need to take occasional
  deep breaths; sighing

- Tingling hands and feet

- Difficulty in
  swallowing

- Pain in chest

- Pain in neck
  and shoulders

- Burping (some-
  times bringing
  fluid with it)

- Irritable bowel—
  gas distension
  of stomach

- Allergies

- Disturbed sleep

- Distorted vision

- Increased sensitivity
  to light and sound

- Ringing in ears
  (tinnitus)

- Increased effect
  of alcohol

- Decrease in pain
  sensation

England, in his article on hyperventilation (Lum, 1981, see Further Reading and Reference, page 125), states that Rice (1950) turned this concept upside down and said that the anxiety was a result of the symptoms and also *that patients could be cured by eliminating faulty breathing.* Lewis (1964) *identified the role of anxiety as a trigger, rather than the prime cause* (my italics).

In another paper on hyperventilation, Lum (1987, see Further Reading and Reference, page 125) also states: "It now must be recognized as a major factor in many neuroses, particularly *panic disorder* and *phobic states*" (my italics).

## Recognizing Hyperventilation

It is easy to recognize someone experiencing severe hyperventilation: you will see erratic, noisy, rapid breaths where the chest is heaving and the abdomen is barely moving. The person feels the need to take an occasional deep breath and often finds it difficult to breathe out. Sighing at intervals seems to relieve this.

*Chronic* hyperventilation is not easy to identify because there is nothing dramatic to see or hear: quiet, shallow rapid breaths with most of the movement from the upper chest.

Often, people are very unwilling to accept that their breathing pattern is causing their symptoms: "My breathing has always been like this—how could it possibly be making me feel so ill?"

Sometimes during a consultation a doctor will encourage her patient to speed up his breathing; the rapid return of his symptoms—tingling, panic, and so on—soon convinces the patient of the source of his troubles.

## How One Develops the Habit of Hyperventilating

There are several triggers: tension, depression, chest troubles, stuffy nose, allergies, wearing tight clothes or a spinal brace, folding arms across chest, physical pain, trying to hold in emotional pain.

# Become Aware of Your Breathing Pattern

It will take time, probably several weeks, for your better breathing to become automatic, so be patient with yourself. To time your breathing rate, look at a wristwatch or clock with a second hand after you have been at rest for about ten minutes. Breathing in and out is one breath: see how many times you do this in 30 seconds, then double it; this will give you the rate you are breathing per minute. If it is 16 or more, you would be wise to follow the exercises below. If you find it difficult to count your breaths, ask a family member to do it when you are unaware of what they are doing. If you find the exercises a bit boring, you could perhaps listen to a favorite soothing program on the radio while doing them. But do them—the results will be worth it.

# Breathing Exercises

These should be slow and gentle, not deep and vigorous. Make the time to do two half-hour sessions daily. If you are having severe symptoms, panic, or agoraphobia (fear of open spaces), a quick five minutes here and there is not enough. The best times are after breakfast and before the evening meal. Sit comfortably in the chair or, better still, lie on the floor or bed, and loosen tight clothing. As you become more skilled you will be able to do this anywhere, even, for instance, standing in a line at the bank.

1. Place one hand on your stomach and one on your chest. The hand on your chest should stay as still as possible. The hand on your stomach will go up and down as you breathe.

2. Breathe out through your nose (don't force it), and let your stomach fall gently as you do so.

3. Breathe in through the nose, letting the stomach rise. Try to make the outward breath longer than the inward breath.

4. Gradually train yourself to breathe between 8 and 12 times per minute.

The aim is to breathe slowly, lifting the abdomen. If you breathe too deeply, you can become lightheaded or your heart may thump a little. This shows that both low carbon dioxide levels *and* a rapid change in these levels can cause symptoms. This is nothing to worry about, but if you get these slight symptoms, just take a rest and start again.

## Panic Attacks—Using Breathing to Cope

If your attitude is, "I will die, be sick, faint, wet myself . . . if I don't fight this panic attack," you will encourage *more* attacks. It will become a trigger for stimulating more adrenaline, and thus more fear. If you teach your body to give the correct messages to your brain, you can break this chain reaction. If your thoughts are panic, panic, panic, they need to be followed by breathe, breathe, breathe. Slow it down.

### First-Aid for Panic Attacks

Since the main cause of the symptoms is too much oxygen buzzing around in you, the aim is to cut the oxygen intake down as quickly as possible. Let your breath out in a long sigh and cup your hands around your nose and mouth to stop your taking in too much oxygen and crowding out the carbon dioxide.

If you are at home you could place a paper—never plastic!—bag around your nose and breathe. Do not blow or breathe deeply into the bag. Just let the breaths come. They will slow down naturally as you get your own carbon dioxide back from the air in the bag. You can also slow the breathing by splashing cold water on your face or putting cold cloths or ice packs over your cheeks and nose. It does not need to be an actual ice pack; a package of frozen peas wrapped in a dish towel, for example, can be very useful.

If breathing is the first thought, what next? This should be: to eat or drink something sweet as soon as possible. Chapter Seventeen explains the importance of maintaining a steady level of sugar in the blood, and how eating sugar is only a first-aid measure for panic and should be followed by a meal and a rest.

For more information on panic attacks, see *Panic Attacks: A Natural Approach* by this author (Ulysses Press, 1999).

# Hypoglycemia and Nerves

## What Is Hypoglycemia?

Hypoglycemia, or low blood sugar, is an abnormally low level of glucose in the blood. The food we eat is turned into glucose by the digestive system, and we use the energy it produces to nourish our bodies, a little like putting gasoline in a car.

Some people think if they eat lots of sugary foods they will be full of energy and the level of glucose (sugar) in their blood will stay normal. This chapter shows that the *opposite* is true, and that it is necessary to cut down on these foods if you have nervous problems.

Hypoglycemia is the opposite of diabetes, a disorder where the pancreas fails to produce the chemical called insulin. Insulin enables us to burn the food we eat to produce energy. The reverse is so in hypoglycemia. The pancreas is overstimulated, usually because of nervous exhaustion, and produces too much insulin. This causes the food we eat to be burned up too quickly and we cannot maintain the levels of blood glucose necessary to function normally.

The results are unpleasant physical effects such as palpitations and feelings of faintness, and because the brain cannot store glucose there are also unpleasant brain effects such as anxiety, depression, panic attacks, and neurotic behavior.

## Is Hypoglycemia an Illness?

Hypoglycemia is not an illness, although there is increasing evidence to show that if it goes unchecked it can predispose you to some chronic illnesses, such as arthritis, ulcers, migraines, allergies, or diabetes. It is common for a person with hypoglycemia to have a family history of these conditions.

But hypoglycemia can be easily cured. All you have to do is revise your eating habits and perhaps slow down.

## Symptoms of Hypoglycemia

Identifying symptoms and treating this problem has changed the lives of many, many people. Their panic attacks have gone, they are no longer tired, their concentration has returned, and the craving for sugary foods, bread, and/or alcohol has disappeared. The most common symptoms of hypoglycemia are listed on page 111.

Some other possible symptoms include: being very dull in the mornings, feeling weak and confused mid-morning or mid-afternoon; wanting something sweet about an hour after main meals, waking between 2 and 3 A.M. feeling hungry and anxious.

Of course, many of the above symptoms can be caused by other conditions. If you do not improve on the diet discussed later in this chapter, then you are unlikely to have a low blood sugar problem and it would be sensible to see your doctor.

## Causes of Hypoglycemia

All of the following can be causes of hypoglycemia: exhausted nerves; underfunction of the pituitary, thyroid, or adrenal glands; severe continuous muscular work; skipping meals; eating too many simple carbohydrate foods (sugar, sweets, chocolate, cakes, cookies, bread); drinking alcohol or sweet drinks; taking drugs including caffeine, nicotine, street drugs, contraceptive pills, steroids, tranquilizers, sleeping pills, and beta-blockers. *Please note:* **Always consult your doctor about cutting down or stopping prescribed drugs.**

You can see from this list that it is relatively easy to disturb your blood sugar levels, and because of this it is a very common problem indeed. It is also on the increase because of the growing numbers of pills swallowed and the amount of junk food eaten. Because the symptoms can be so dramatic, it is often mistaken for more serious conditions, and, in the same way as those with symptoms of hyperventilation, people are often subjected unnecessarily to a lot of tests.

It could be argued that every emotion has a physical "twin," and as with hyperventilation it is another chicken-and-egg situation. Does the hypoglycemia follow the exhausted nerves—or is it the other way around? There is a great deal of evidence to show that it is *much* more usual for the physical changes to precede the emotional changes (mood swings, panic attacks, and so forth), and if you think about this, it makes more sense this way. A disturbance in metabolism (body chemistry) is bound to cause personality changes.

## Hypoglycemia as a Cause of Panic Attacks

Panic attacks are by far the most distressing symptoms of hypoglycemia. This is how they happen:

The digestion of well-balanced meals keeps the blood sugar stable. In the absence of food, the blood sugar falls and in order to keep our nervous system, muscles, and the like, functioning we have to call on our "reserve tank," the glucose that is stored in the liver. The stomach cries "Help, the tank is empty!" and the brain responds by sending a chemical messenger (yes, adrenaline) to release the stored food (glucose) in the liver. Unfortunately, as we have seen throughout this book, too much adrenaline causes many unpleasant feelings, including panic attacks.

People are often very stubborn about accepting that they are causing their panic attacks by the way they're eating—or not eating. They also

# The Most Common
# Symptoms of Hypoglycemia

- Blurred vision
- Headaches
- Fainting
- Epilepsy
- Migraines
- Drowsiness
- Fatigue
- Insomnia
- Jaundiced look
- Irritability
- Poor concentration
- Panic feelings
- Lack of coordination
- Alcoholism
- Hyperactivity
- Free-floating anxiety
- Depression
- Asthma
- Indigestion
- Chest pain
- Palpitations
- Feelings of inner trembling
- Constant hunger
- Overacid stomach
- Obesity
- Food cravings
- Excessive smoking
- Allergies
- Premenstrual tension
- Lack of sex drive
- Cold hands and feet
- Stiff muscles
- Stiff joints
- Swollen feet

find it difficult to grasp that if they eat a diet high in refined carbohy-drates (lots of sweet foods, cereals, white bread, and so on), it can often be worse than missing a meal.

## Some Reasons

In the chapter on hyperventilation, we said that the carbon dioxide level in the blood does not need to be way below normal for severe symptoms such as panic to develop; a sudden drop, even if it doesn't go below normal, can cause big trouble. It is the same with blood sugar levels; the change is the important factor. It is well documented that full-scale panic attacks and other symptoms can occur when the level is only on the lower end of the normal scale.

If you eat sugary foods, particularly when you are very hungry, the pancreas (which is already jittery and in top gear) pushes out more insulin than is necessary to cope with the sugar. The result is a rapid drop in blood sugar levels followed by a flood of adrenaline.

## Some Examples

June came in to the group therapy session very tearful, saying she had just had a panic attack and it could not have been low blood sugar because she had stopped for lunch. When it was revealed that "lunch" was toast and a Danish pastry with two cups of black coffee, plus a cigarette, the other group members could see what she had done. They helped her to see the pattern of her attacks: Thursday nights, Friday mornings, and Sunday early evenings. On Thursday she has a night out with the girls—two gin and tonics followed by coffee and chocolate cake. During the week her evening meal is a "proper" meal, but on Sunday she has sandwiches, French toast, pies, and cakes with her mother. When she changed to one glass of dry white wine with cheese and unsweetened crackers (such as Ryvita) for Thursday eve-ning, and a tuna salad with whole-grain bread on Sunday, her panic attacks disappeared.

*Note:* If you make your blood sugar unstable, it may not affect you until the next day or the middle of the night.

Ryan had been having panic attacks for seven months. They started when he gave up smoking. He was anxious to try the low-blood sugar method of eating, because he had already suspected missing meals was the trigger for his migraines. After four weeks he was confident he had found the cause of his trouble. He had only suffered three panic attacks; they were much milder than the ones he had previously experienced, and two came after drinking beer and postponing his evening meal. His headaches had lessened as well.

## Who Is Likely to Have a Hypoglycemia Problem?

Everyone will experience some degree of hypoglycemia sometime in their lives. Have you ever seen an irritable, tearful young child become happy and relaxed as soon as she has eaten, or felt your mind clear and the shaky feeling inside leave you, after you have a mid-morning break? (A large part of the misery of a hangover is also due to low blood sugar.)

Dieters, athletes, and nervous people are most likely to have severe symptoms of hypoglycemia.

## Addiction and Hypoglycemia

Many drugs, including alcohol, nicotine, tranquilizers, and sleeping pills, artificially raise the blood sugar levels. When the level of the drug in the blood drops, the blood sugar also falls. There is often a confusion between symptoms of drug withdrawal and hypoglycemia, because they both include headache, anxiety, depression, and shaking. While it is difficult to separate the symptoms, it is certainly very clear that people withdrawing from drugs who keep to a hypoglycemic diet plan, not only dramatically reduce their withdrawal symptoms, but are also much more likely to complete withdrawal and not feel the need to turn to other substances. For example, people withdrawing from alcohol often turn to tranquilizers, and vice versa.

It is very important for people in withdrawal who come from families where there are other hypoglycemia problems (asthma, arthritis, allergies) to follow the hypoglycemic diet plan. It is also wise to start the diet three or four weeks before you intend to stop smoking or drinking, or before you cut down the dose of tranquilizers or sleeping pills.

# The Hypoglycemic Diet

The following plan will keep blood sugar levels stable. *Note:* If your doctor has already given you a diet to follow, consult her before you change to this one.

## *Principles of the Diet*

The aim is to avoid foods and substances that are quickly absorbed, in order to minimize rapid changes of glucose levels in the blood.

### CARBOHYDRATES

*Avoid or cut down to a minimum refined carbohydrates:* These include sugar, sweets, chocolate, white bread, white flour, cakes, cookies, pastries, alcohol, sweet drinks, junk food.

*Eat nonrefined (complex) carbohydrates:* These include whole-grain cereals —wheat, oats, barley, rice, rye, millet.

Give up processed breakfast cereals (which contain a lot of sugars) and make your own muesli from whole oats, nuts, seeds (sunflower, pumpkin, or sesame are all very nutritious), and a little dried fruit (raisins, apricots, figs). If you are used to eating "plastic" bread, you will love the taste of whole-grain brown bread, and if you normally eat brown bread make sure it is whole grain.

### PROTEIN

There is a fair amount of disagreement on how much protein should be included in any diet. The early diets for low blood sugar were very high in protein. Eating this way controls the blood sugar, but more recent research has shown that the body does not like too much concentrated protein. Blood sugar levels can be kept steady on smaller amounts of protein, especially if plenty of raw vegetables are included.

Animal protein: meat, fish, poultry, cheese, eggs, milk, yogurt.

Vegetable protein: nuts, seeds, peas, beans, lentils, soy, and possibly small amounts in all vegetables.

## VEGETABLES AND FRUIT

*Eat large quantities of vegetables:* These will supply you with essential minerals and vitamins and will also provide needed roughage. Some people have become overanxious about roughage—bran with everything. This is not a good idea, as it can irritate the bowel and hinder the absorption of some minerals. Eating vegetables is a better way to get roughage.

*Eat lots of fresh fruit:* Although fruit contains quite a lot of sugar, it is in a different form (fructose); it does not need insulin for its digestion. Therefore it is an ideal food to help slow down the pancreas.

## FAT

Not all fats are bad. People tend to worry too much about cholesterol levels when saturated fat (which tends to be solid at room temperature) is more of an issue. Next time you are about to spread your bread with some tasteless margarine (which is probably full of nasty additives anyway), remind yourself that worrying and not eating raw vegetables and fruit can be just as damaging as moderate amounts of butter. Also remember that some foods, including onions, garlic, apples, and olive oil, actually lower your cholesterol levels. Olive oil is also wonderful for the immune system, the body's defense against disease.

## The Diet

*As soon as you get up or while still in bed:*

A 4-ounce glass of unsweetened juice, half a grapefruit, or a medium orange

*Breakfast:*

More fruit juice or fruit and choose from:

Cooked breakfast: bacon, eggs, ham, cottage cheese, or any other protein dish, plus any vegetable, such as tomatoes or mushrooms (perhaps in an omelette); one slice of whole-grain bread, two flatbreads, rice cakes with butter or margarine *or*

Oatmeal sweetened with a few raisins or muesli made from whole cereals, nuts, and seeds (pumpkin, sunflower) or plain yogurt with fresh fruit and nuts. You can flavor this with spices: cinnamon, ginger, crushed cardamom

Weak tea or one cup weak coffee, with milk if desired

*Two hours after breakfast:*

A snack of fruit, yogurt, nuts, milk

*Lunch:*

Any protein dish: hot or cold meat, tuna or other fish, cheese, eggs, chicken, or any lentil, bean, or nut dish. All to be eaten with lots of salad or vegetables, one slice of whole-grain bread or two flatbreads

*Two-and-a-half to three hours after lunch or earlier:*

Weak tea or milk, with flatbread, cottage cheese, and patê or all-fruit jam

*One-half to one hour before dinner:*

4 ounces of fruit juice

*Dinner:*

Same as lunch plus fruit, flatbread and butter with cottage cheese, weak herbal tea

This diet plan might look like a lot of food, but remember there is no need to eat large quantities—small and often is the rule.

Try not to make a new way of eating another of life's stresses. As your symptoms improve, you can add treats like a glass of dry white wine or a piece of cake. Many people really crave sugar at first and experience aches and pains and other withdrawal feelings. These go away after a few days. Other people also say that, eating this way, they have more energy than they have had for years. And when they try to go back to their old eating habits after their nerves have improved, they often find they have lost their taste for junk food and miss the clean taste of vegetables and fruit.

# Hypoglycemia from Any Cause

Arthritis                                                Fatigue, headaches

Allergies                                                Shaking inside

Overeating,                                 Diagnosed as nerves;
poor general health                       pills or talking therapy

More stress                                              Depression

Search for other
solutions: drink, overdependence
on people, etc.

The circle of misdiagnosed hypoglycemia

## Dos and Don'ts

- ◆ Don't skip meals.

- ◆ Eat regularly.

- ◆ Avoid white flour and sugary foods and drinks.

- ◆ Cut down on caffeine, cigarettes, and alcohol.

- ◆ Always have protein in your breakfast.

- ◆ Never eat a starch-only meal (bread, cake, cereal).

## Being Overweight

If you are overweight, you should lose weight with this eating plan because it does not include a lot of carbohydrates. If this does not happen, you could try excluding all grains or cutting down on the quantities at each meal, but continue to eat at the same times. *Remember:* you will not lose weight by going for long periods between meals. This will make you crave all the foods you should not have. If your weight is still not coming down after a few weeks, see your doctor; there may be another reason for your being overweight, such as an underactive thyroid.

## Being Underweight

Some people who have had a high sugar and fat diet lose weight at first on this eating plan before starting to gain. If you want to put on weight, eat more potatoes, bread, rice, and milk drinks and slow down. Your weight should improve. A persistent weight loss should always be reported to your doctor, but do give yourself time for your body to adjust to this way of eating.

# CHAPTER EIGHTEEN

# What About the Spirit?

*A cheerful heart is good medicine but a crushed spirit dries up
the bones.*
                                                    —*Proverbs 22*

I find it difficult to talk about depression without mention of the spirit—
after all, we talk about being "low-spirited" when we are "gray" or
"blue," and though many reasons for depression have been discussed in
this book, I feel that for many people this state may come from a background of fear, an often unconscious state of being in continual fear.
Much of this could be fear of death, of extinction, of being snuffed out
like a candle, perhaps with the feeling that life is finite and that you
have to strive to experience all, because there is only one chance. I do
not believe this. I believe we take with us into the next world—a
world much happier than this—all that we need: love and learning.

## What Is the Spirit?

My feeling is that the spirit is a part of our consciousness that, when
we are born, stays in Heaven, the Universe, or however you choose to
call it; and this is our Divine spark. It is the part of us that prompts us

to love and learn and progress spiritually, probably through many lifetimes, toward the Godhead. We hurt our soul by not loving ourselves, by not listening to the information in our dreams, and by seeing the pains of life as terrible misfortunes instead of as the tools we selected, before we were born, to carve out our chosen path. Salvation comes when we learn to forgive and love ourselves as vulnerable human beings. Only when we do this can the memories be healed, can we be freed from negative emotions, and can we treat those around us with the same gentleness with which we treat ourselves.

I believe there are many roads to the Divine. Although I consider myself a Christian, there are many Christians who would dispute this, because I respect and embrace parts of other faiths and philosophies as well. For me, a Hereafter populated only by Christians would be a denial of Unconditional Love.

I hope you will understand, in the following two poems, that I can only write from my own images and faith. If you take the essence of them and interpret them in the Light of your own prophets and faith, I hope they will "speak" to you.

The first one expresses what so many depressed people say: "I know I am here but I am not living; the fall arrives and I think, 'What happened to spring and summer?' " I hope you will feel less alone with those feelings when you know how common they are in depression.

The second poem expresses how many people have found a way forward by changing useless thought patterns, forgiving themselves and others, and connecting with their inner life. A helpful book on this is *Feel the Fear and Do It Anyway: How to Turn Your Fear and Indecision into Confidence and Action*, by Susan Jeffers (Arrow, 1991).

### Reasonless Seasons

If the meter peters out
Where's the rhyme or reason?
The seasons come and go
With the ebb but not the flow . . .

There's nothing in the store,
The shore is strewn with life's litter.

Spring showers fail to nourish;
To bring the promised flourish.
A harsh summer sun desiccates the bones.
They take their place amongst the stones.
Bleached-white
In the dried brine
Of the tide-line.

Can there be any knowing?
Can there be any growing?
Walking bent and spent
In the raining and the snowing.

There is no choice;
Continue with the charade,
Promenade in new clothes,
With fixed smile.
While away the time
Until true spring showers,
Made fertile by the life-blood
Of the Gentle Jew,
Penetrate the parched plains
And push skyward from the mud
Green shoots of hope, of life, of love.

### Looking for a New Song

Sing the song of the happy child.
He's waiting without to come in.

Sing the song of the fairy child.
He'll dance with you in a ring.

Sing the song of the old soul
Who has lived long and learnt to be free.
He has gained from the pain
And is joyful again,
Just as he ought to be.

Hark to the song of the high hills,
Of rivers and rushing streams.
Eavesdrop at night when starlight is bright
To the wisdom and promptings of dreams.

Cling to the back of the night owl;
He'll help you toward your goal.
Lay your head on his neck,
Don't keep him in check:
He'll take you to meet your soul.

Feel the beat of your own heart.
Take time to be quiet and still.
Hear the drum of the man's heart,
A man who has choice and free will . . .
Then, thrill to the beat of another heart
Pulsating within your own.

The loving beat of the other heart
Makes strong the sounds of the first.
It belongs to the Man who on Calvary
Forgave; as He said, "I thirst."

In the hope that something in these pages has been of help to you and
that you will find Peace and Light in your journey through life.

# Quick References to Combat Depression and Anxiety

## Depression

1—Move. Get your circulation going.

2—Don't lie in bed; get up at the same time each day (9 a.m. at the latest).

3—Even if you can't do much, do something; you can finish it the next day.

4—Eat regular meals; eat good food.

5—Try to walk 20 minutes in the brightest part of the day; don't wear your sunglasses. If you can't face walking, sit by an open window.

6—Build up exercise; force leaden limbs to move; use breathing exercises.

7—Go to bed early.

Every day in every way, you are getting better and better.
Believe it. It works!

## Anxiety

1—Slow down.

2—Have a short relaxation before eating—regular meals, good food.

3—Rest in the middle of the day.

4—Use breathing exercises.

5—Have plenty of fresh air, and get outdoor exercise if possible.

6—Use positive self-talk.

7—Go to bed early.

# Further Reading and Reference

Balch, James F., M.D., and Balch, Phyllis A., M.D., *Prescription for Nutritional Healing* (Avery Publishing Group, 1997).

Barlow, Wilfred, *The Alexander Principle* (Arrow, 1975). To find your nearest qualified Alexander Teacher, contact the North American Society of Teachers of the Alexander Technique (NASTAT) at 800-474-0626.

Blackwood, John, and Fulder, Stephen, *Garlic—Nature's Original Remedy* (Healing Arts Press, 1991).

Chaitow, Leon, *Candida Albicans: Is Yeast Your Problem?* (Thorsons, 1987).

Crook, William, M.D., and Jones, Marjorie Hurt R.N., *The Yeast Connection Cookbook* (Professional Books, 1999).

Cutler, Howard C., M.D., and The Dalai Lama, *The Art of Happiness* (Riverhead Books, 1998).

Davies, Stephen, and Stewart, Alan, *Nutritional Medicine* (Pan, 1986).

Dawes, Belinda, and Downing, Damien, *Why M.E.?* (Grafton, 1989). Clear and practical guidelines for coping with ME, written by two doctors, one of who suffers from the disease. For further information on

ME write to the ME Association, P.O. Box 8, Stanford le Hope, Essex, U.K. SS17 8EX or call the CFIDS Association in Charlotte, North Carolina at 800-44-CFIDS.

Dement, William, M.D., *The Promise of Sleep* (Lively Planet Press, 1999).

DesMaisons, Kathleen, Ph.D., *Potatoes Not Prozac* (Fireside, 1999).

Dickson, Ann, *A Woman in Your Own Right: Assertiveness and You* (Quartet, 1988).

Downing, Damien, *Daylight Robbery—The Importance of Sunlight to Health* (Arrow, 1988).

Garrison, Robert Jr. and Somer, Elizabeth, *The Nutrition Desk Reference* (Keats Publishing, 1995).

Grant, Doris, and Joice, Jean, *Food Combining for Health* (Thorsons, 1986).

Kircher, Tamara, and Lowery, Penny, *Herbal Remedies* (Macmillan, 1996).

Lum, L. C., "Hyperventilation and Anxiety State," *Journal of the Royal Society of Medicine*, vol. 74 (January, 1981).

———"Hyperventilation Syndromes in Medicine & Psychiatry: A Review," *Journal of the Royal Society of Medicine*, vol. 80 (April, 1987).

Maleskey, Gail and the editors of "Prevention," *Nature's Medicines* (Rodale Press, 1999).

Pierpaoli, Walter, and Regelson, William, *The Melatonin Miracle* (Fourth Estate, 1996).

Powell, John, *Why Am I Afraid to Tell You Who I Am?* (Fontana, 1975).

———*Unconditional Love* (Argus, 1978).

———*Why Am I Afraid to Love?* (Argus, 1978).

Ramsay, Melvin, *Post-Viral Syndrome—The Saga of the Royal Free Disease* (ME Association [see address above, under "Dawes"], 1988).

Schardt, David, "St. John's Worts and All," *Nutrition Action*, vol. 27, no. 7 (September, 2000).

Tisser, Maggie, *The Art of Aromatherapy* (Thorsons, 1986). For further information on aromatherapy, write to the International Federation of Aromatherapists, 46 Dalkeith Road, London, U.K. SE21.

Trickett, Shirley, *Free Yourself from Tranquilizers and Sleeping Pills* (Ulysses Press, 1997).

———*The Irritable Bowel Syndrome and Diverticulosis* (Thorsons, 1990).

———*Coping with Candida* (Sheldon Press, 1994).

———*Recipes for Health: Candida Albicans Yeast-Free and Sugar-Free Recipes* (Thorsons, 1994).

———*Coping with Candida* (Sheldon Press, 1994).

Waesse, Harry, *Yoga for Beginners* (Sterling Publishing Co., 1999).

Weekes, Claire, *Good Night, Good Morning; Moving to Freedom; Going on Holiday; Nervous Fatigue—Understanding and Coping with it; Hope and Help for Your Nerves.* These tapes and very useful leaflets on relaxation are available from: Relaxation for Living, Dunesk, 29 Burwood Park Road, Walton on Thames, Surrey, U.K., KT12 5LH.

Weil, Andrew, M.D., *Eight Weeks to Optimal Health* (Alfred A. Knopf, 1998).

———*Spontaneous Healing* (Alfred A. Knopf, 1995).

Wright, Celia, *The Wright Diet* (Grafton, 1989).

# Guidelines for the Use of Tranquilizers and Sleeping Pills

## USES

### As Anxiolytics [Anxiety-relieving drugs]

1. Benzodiazepines are indicated for the short-term relief (two to four weeks only) of anxiety that is severe, disabling, or subjecting the individual to unacceptable distress, occurring alone or in association with insomnia or short-term psychosomatic organic or psychotic illness.

2. The use of benzodiazepines to treat short-term "mild" anxiety is inappropriate and unsuitable.

### As Hypnotics [Sleep-Inducing Drugs]

3. Benzodiazepines should be used to treat insomnia only when it is severe, disabling, or subjecting the individual to extreme distress.

DOSE

1. *The lowest dose which can control the symptoms should be used. It should not be continued beyond four weeks.*

2. *Long-term chronic use is not recommended.*

3. *Treatment should always be tapered off gradually.*

4. *Patients who have taken benzodiazepines for a long time may require a longer period during which doses are reduced.*

5. *When a benzodiazepine is used as a hypnotic, treatment should, if possible, be intermittent.*

PRECAUTIONS

1. *Benzodiazepines should not be used alone to treat depression or anxiety associated with depression. Suicide may be precipitated in such patients.*

2. *They should not be used for phobic or obsessional states.*

3. *They should not be used for the treatment of chronic psychosis.*

4. *In case of loss or bereavement, psychological adjustment may be inhibited by benzodiazepines.*

5. *Disinhibiting effects may be manifested in various ways. Suicide may be precipitated in patients who are depressed, and aggressive behavior toward self and others may be precipitated. Extreme caution should therefore be used in prescribing benzodiazepines in patients with personality disorders.*

## Benzodiazepines Withdrawal Symptoms

*Withdrawal symptoms include anxiety, tremor, confusion, insomnia, perception disorders, fits, depression, gastrointestinal, and other somatic symptoms. These may sometimes be difficult to distinguish from the symptoms of the original illness.*

*It is important to note that withdrawal symptoms can occur with benzodiazepines following therapeutic doses given for short periods of time.*

*Withdrawal effects usually appear shortly after stopping a benzodiazepine with a short half-life. Symptoms may continue for weeks or months. No epidemiological evidence is available to suggest that one benzodiazepine is more responsible for the development of dependency or withdrawal symptoms than another. The Committee on Safety of Medicines recommends that the use of benzodiazepines should be limited as discussed in the uses and precautions listed on pages 128–29.*

From "Current Problems" (Committee on Safety of Medicines), No. 21, January 1988

## Long-acting Benzodiazepines

Chlorazepate (Tranxene)

Chlordiazepoxide (Librium)

Clonazepam (Klonopin)

Diazepam (Valium, Valrelease)

Flurazepam (Dalmane)

Halezapam (Paxipam)

Quazepam (Doral)

## Medium-acting Benzodiazepines

Lorazepam (Ativan)

Temazepam (Restoril)

## Short-acting Benzodiazepines

Alprazolom (Xanax)

Estazolam (Prosom)

Midazolam (Versed)

Oxazepam (Serax)

Triazolam (Halcion)

# Guidelines for Withdrawal from Antidepressants

In Chapter Eleven, we discussed the newer types of antidepressant medication—the SSRIs and tricyclics, and, less commonly, the MAOIs—now being prescribed. The treatment guidelines for depression offer information on diagnosis, establishment and maintenance of drug therapy for all these antidepressants. Very little is offered, though, about how to discontinue their use and deal with withdrawal symptoms.

Symptoms of antidepressant withdrawal may occur one or more days after discontinuing use of the medication and last a week or longer. Symptoms include flulike reactions, nausea and stomach upset, insomnia, dizziness, confusion, nightmares, hallucinations, palpitations, and anxiety. The longer a drug has been taken and the higher the dose, the more likely withdrawal symptoms will occur. Symptoms are also greater if the medication is stopped too abruptly. (Note that just because you have withdrawal symptoms does not mean the drug is addictive.)

To limit withdrawal symptoms, do the following:

• Never stop taking antidepressants suddenly. If you did stop suddenly, you may need to start taking them again and then taper off.

• Talk to your doctor and pharmacist about slowly tapering off.

(One type of tapering schedule reduces the medication 25% each week for four weeks, but learn what's best for the medication you're taking.)

# Referral List

AMERICAN MENTAL HEALTH COUNSELORS
801 North Fairfax Street, Suite 304
Alexandria, VA 22314
(800) 326-2642
www.amhca.org
Call or write for referral information about counselors in your area.

AMERICAN PSYCHIATRIC ASSOCIATION
Public Affairs Office, Suite 501
1400 K Street NW
Washington, DC 20005
(888) 357-7924
www.psych.org
For referral information about psychiatrists in your area, call or
write the APA Public Affairs office.

AMERICAN PSYCHOLOGICAL ASSOCIATION
750 First Street, N.E.
Washington, DC 20002
(202) 336-5800
www.helping.apa.org
Contact for referral information about psychologists in your area.

ANXIETY DISORDERS ASSOCIATION OF AMERICA
11900 Parklawn Drive, Suite 100
Rockville, MD 20852
(301) 231-9350
www.adaa.org
Call or write to receive a list of mental health professionals who
treat anxiety disorders and a list of self-help groups in your area.

FREEDOM FROM FEAR
308 Seaview Avenue
Staten Island, NY 10305
(718) 351-1717
www.freedomfromfear.org
Call or write for a free newsletter on anxiety disorders and a referral
list of treatment specialists.

NATIONAL ANXIETY FOUNDATION
3135 Custer Drive
Lexington, KY 40517-4001
(606) 272-7166
www.lexington-on-line.com/naf.html
NAF provides referrals to their members and other mental health
professionals around the country.

NATIONAL DEPRESSIVE AND MANIC-DEPRESSIVE
ASSOCIATION
730 North Franklin, Suite 501
Chicago, IL 60610
(800) 826-3632
www.ndmda.org
Call or write for a list of support groups in your area.

NATIONAL INSTITUTE OF MENTAL HEALTH
Public Inquiries
6001 Executive Boulevard, Room 8184, MSC 9663
Bethesda, MD 20892
(301) 443-4513
www.nimh.nih.gov

NATIONAL MENTAL HEALTH ASSOCIATION
(800) 969-6642
www.nmha.org

OBSESSIVE COMPULSIVE FOUNDATION
337 Notch Hill Road
North Branford, CT 06471
(203) 315-2190
www.ocfoundation.org
Call or write for a list of mental health practitioners in your area
who specialize in treating OCD.

# Index

# Ulysses Press Mind/Body Books

## A Natural Approach Books

Written in a friendly, nontechnical style, *A Natural Approach* books address specific health issues and show you how to take an active part in your own treatment. Believing that disease is more than a combination of symptoms, these books offer integrated mind/body programs that take a positive, preventative approach.

CANDIDA
Shirley Trickett & Karen Brody,
$11.95

IRRITABLE BOWEL SYNDROME
2nd edition, Rosemary Nicol,
$13.95

ENDOMETRIOSIS
Jo Mears, $9.95

MIGRAINES
Sue Dyson, $10.95

FREE YOURSELF FROM TRANQUILIZERS
& SLEEPING PILLS
Shirley Trickett, $9.95

PANIC ATTACKS
2nd edition, Shirley Trickett, $9.95

IRRITABLE BLADDER & INCONTINENCE
Jennifer Hunt, $8.95

## Other Mind/Body Titles

GIVE YOUR FACE A LIFT: NATURAL WAYS TO LOOK AND FEEL GOOD
Penny Stanway, $17.95
This full-color guide to natural face care tells how to give oneself a "natural facelift" using oils, creams, masks and homemade products that nourish and beautify the skin.

HEALING REIKI: REUNITE MIND, BODY AND SPIRIT WITH HEALING ENERGY
Eleanor McKenzie, $16.95
Examines the meaning, attitudes and history of Reiki while providing practical tips for receiving and giving this universal life energy.

HERBS THAT WORK: THE SCIENTIFIC EVIDENCE OF THEIR HEALING POWERS
David Armstrong, $12.95
Unlike herb books relying on folklore or vague anecdotes, *Herbs that Work* is the first consumer guide to rate herbal remedies based on documented, state-of-the-art scientific research.

HOW MEDITATION HEALS: A PRACTICAL GUIDE TO IMPROVING
YOUR HEALTH AND WELL-BEING
Eric Harrison, $12.95
Combines Eastern wisdom with medical and scientific evidence to explain how and why meditation improves the functioning of all systems of the body.

HOW TO MEDITATE: AN ILLUSTRATED GUIDE TO CALMING THE MIND AND RELAXING THE BODY
Paul Roland, $16.95
Offers a friendly, illustrated approach to calming the mind and raising consciousness through various techniques, including basic meditation, visualization, body scanning for tension, affirmations and mantras.

THE JOSEPH H. PILATES METHOD AT HOME:
A BALANCE, SHAPE, STRENGTH & FITNESS PROGRAM
Eleanor McKenzie, $16.95
This handbook describes and details Pilates, a mental and physical program that combines elements of yoga and classical dance.

KNOW YOUR BODY: THE ATLAS OF ANATOMY
2nd edition, Introduction by Emmet B. Keeffe, M.D., $14.95
Provides a comprehensive, full-color guide to the human body.

NEW AGAIN!: THE 28-DAY DETOX PLAN FOR BODY AND SOUL
Anna Selby, $16.95
Allows you to free your body *and* mind from toxins and live a healthy and balanced life.

SENSES WIDE OPEN: THE ART AND PRACTICE OF LIVING IN YOUR BODY
Johanna Putnoi, $14.95
Through simple, accessible exercises, this book shows how to be at ease with yourself and experience genuine pleasure in your physical connection to others and the world.

THE 7 HEALING CHAKRAS: UNLOCKING YOUR BODY'S ENERGY CENTERS
Brenda Davies, $14.95
Explores the essence of chakras, vortices of energy that connect the physical body with the spiritual.

SIMPLY RELAX: AN ILLUSTRATED GUIDE TO SLOWING DOWN AND ENJOYING LIFE
Dr. Sarah Brewer, $15.95
In a beautifully illustrated format, this book clearly presents physical and mental disciplines that show readers how to relax.

WEEKEND HOME SPA: FOUR CREATIVE ESCAPES—CLEANSING, ENERGIZING, RELAXING AND PAMPERING
Linda Bird, $16.95
Shows how to create that spa experience in your own home with step-by-step mini workouts, stretching routines, meditations and visualizations, as well as more challenging exercises to boost mental potential.

---

*To order these books call 800-377-2542 or 510-601-8301, fax 510-601-8307, e-mail ulysses@ulyssespress.com, or write to Ulysses Press, P.O. Box 3440, Berkeley, CA 94703. All retail orders are shipped free of charge. California residents must include sales tax. Allow two to three weeks for delivery.*

# About the Author

Shirley Trickett trained as a nurse before becoming a counselor and teacher. She is based in the northeast of England and travels both throughout the United Kingdom and abroad with her work. Trickett has assisted anxious and depressed people for many years. She is the author of *Candida: A Natural Approach* (Ulysses Press, 1999), *Panic Attacks: A Natural Approach* (Ulysses Press, 1999), *Free Yourself from Tranquilizers and Sleeping Pills* (Ulysses Press, 1997), *Headaches and Migraine* (Penguin, 1996), and *The Irritable Bowel Syndrome and Diverticulosis* (Thorsons, 1990). In 1987 she won a Whitbread Community Care Award for her work.